Options Mastery: Navigating the Financial Frontier

Alex Thompson

Published by Side Hustle Success, 2023.

OPTIONS MASTERY: NAVIGATING THE FINANCIAL FRONTIER

First edition. September 28, 2023.

ISBN: 979-8223661993

Written by Alex Thompson.

Also by Alex Thompson

Alex on Finance

Financial Freedom Roadmap - Achieving Early Retirement through the FIRE Movement

The Art of Strategic Innovation

Beyond Cash - The Evolution of Digital Payment Systems and the Future of Money

Preserving Wealth in Inflationary Times - Strategies for Protecting Your Financial Future

Standalone

Side Hustle Success: Unlocking Your Entrepreneurial Potential

Side Hustle Success: The Ultimate Guide to Passive and Financial Freedom

Mastering the Markets: Advanced Trading Strategies for Success and Ethical Trading Practices

Financial Fortitude

Mastering the Art of Upselling

The Financial Bullet Blueprint

Investing Demystified: A Beginner's Guide to Building Wealth in the Stock Market

Real Estate Riches: Building Wealth through Property Investment

How To Succeed as a Freelancer

Navigating Complex Waters: Advanced Strategies in Portfolio Management
Behavioral Finance and Investor Psychology
Leading with Empathy: Harnessing Emotional Intelligence for Effective Leadership
Financial Independence
Thriving Within Your Means: A Guide to Affordable Living
Algorithmic Trading: Navigating the Digital Frontier
Navigating Alternative Investments
Navigating the Behavioral Finance Landscape
Unlocking the Power of Derivatives
Mastering International Finance
Quantitative Finance and Risk Modeling
Sustainable and ESG Investing
Options Mastery: Navigating the Financial Frontier
Portfolio Mastery: Navigating the Financial Art and Science

Table of Contents

To all those who dare to dream, analyze, strategize, and ultimately thrive in the exhilarating world of options trading. Your pursuit of financial mastery is an inspiration to us all.

Chapter 1: Introduction to Options

Basics of Option Contracts (Calls and Puts)

In the world of finance, options are indispensable tools that provide investors and traders with an array of strategies for managing risk, speculating on price movements, and generating income. These financial instruments come in two primary forms: call options and put options. In this introductory chapter, we will explore the fundamental concepts of call and put options, shedding light on their definitions, key features, and core principles.

Call Options: Capitalizing on Upside Potential

Definition: A **call option** is a financial contract that grants the holder the right, but not the obligation, to purchase an underlying asset at a predetermined price, known as the **strike price**, on or before a specified expiration date. Call options are widely utilized when investors anticipate an increase in the price of the underlying asset.

Key Concepts in Call Options:

1. **Strike Price**: Central to any call option is the strike price. It serves as the fixed price at which the option holder is entitled to buy the underlying asset. For instance, if an investor possesses a call option with a strike price of $100 for a particular stock, they have the prerogative to buy that stock at $100 per share, regardless of its current market value.

2. **Expiration Date**: All option contracts come with an expiration date, marking the point at which the contract becomes void. Post this date, the option holder loses the right to exercise the option. The time remaining until expiration is a critical consideration when trading call options.

3. **Profit Potential**: Call options offer profit potential when the price of the underlying asset rises above the strike price. The more the asset's price exceeds the strike price, the greater the potential profit for the call option holder.

4. **Limited Risk**: One of the principal advantages of buying call options is the limited risk they entail. The maximum loss the investor can incur is equal to the premium paid for the option. This premium represents the cost of acquiring the call option.

5. **Speculation and Leverage**: Call options are a favored choice for speculation due to their inherent leverage. They enable investors to control a more substantial position in the underlying asset with a relatively modest investment. While this leverage can magnify profits when the market moves in the expected direction, it also heightens the risk of losses.

Put Options: Safeguarding Against Downside Risk

Definition: In contrast to call options, **put options** grant investors the right, but not the obligation, to sell an underlying asset at a predetermined strike price on or before a specified expiration date. These options are primarily utilized when investors anticipate a decline in the price of the underlying asset.

Key Concepts in Put Options:

1. **Strike Price**: As with call options, put options are defined by the strike price, which determines the price at which the option holder can sell the underlying asset. For instance, if an investor holds a put option with a strike price of $50 for a specific stock, they have the right to sell that stock at $50 per share, irrespective of its current market price.

2. **Expiration Date**: Put options are also bound by an expiration date, signaling the termination of the option contract. This date should be a crucial consideration when trading put options.

3. **Profit Potential**: Put options offer the potential for profit if the price of the underlying asset falls below the strike price. The greater the decline in the asset's price, the higher the potential profit for the put option holder.

4. **Limited Risk**: Similar to call options, buying put options confines the investor's risk to the premium paid for the option. This premium represents the maximum loss the investor can sustain.

5. **Risk Management and Hedging**: Put options find extensive use in risk management and hedging. Investors can utilize them as insurance against potential declines in the value of their portfolios. If the market experiences a downturn, gains from put options can offset losses in the portfolio.

This chapter lays the groundwork for comprehending the intricacies of options. The knowledge of call and put options forms the basis for an extensive array of trading and investment strategies, each tailored to specific financial objectives. In the forthcoming chapters, we will delve deeper into the complexities of options, exploring advanced strategies and gaining deeper insights into the dynamic world of financial markets.

Historical Development of Options Markets

To fully grasp the intricacies of options, it is essential to appreciate their historical development. The evolution of options markets over centuries has been marked by innovation, adaptation to changing financial landscapes, and the emergence of diverse contract types. In this chapter, we embark on a journey through time to explore the rich history of options markets, tracing their origins, key milestones, and contributions to modern finance.

The Origins of Options: Ancient Beginnings

The roots of options can be traced back to ancient civilizations, where rudimentary forms of option contracts were employed for various purposes:

1. **Ancient Greece**: The earliest recorded options-like contracts can be found in ancient Greek city-states, where olive oil traders used agreements resembling call options. These contracts granted the buyer the right to purchase olive oil at a specified future date.

2. **Ancient Rome**: Roman merchants engaged in similar practices, using contracts that resembled modern-day futures and options contracts. These agreements allowed parties to lock in prices for goods to be delivered in the future.

Medieval Europe: Emergence of Early Option-Like Contracts

During the Middle Ages, Europe witnessed the emergence of contracts that bore similarities to contemporary options:

1. **Put Options in Bruges**: In medieval Bruges, traders and merchants engaged in put option-like transactions. A seller would pay a premium for the right to sell goods back to the original seller at a predetermined price if the market price fell.

2. **Amsterdam Stock Exchange**: In the 17th century, the Amsterdam Stock Exchange was home to early options trading. Dutch investors used "tulip options" to speculate on the prices of tulip bulbs, which were highly sought after during the famous "Tulip Mania."

18th and 19th Centuries: Agricultural Origins

The agricultural sector played a significant role in shaping the development of options markets during the 18th and 19th centuries:

1. **Chicago Board of Trade**: In the 19th century, the Chicago Board of Trade (CBOT) played a pivotal role in options history by offering standardized options contracts on agricultural commodities such as corn and wheat. These early options were designed to provide farmers and traders with price protection.

2. **Options in London**: Options trading also gained momentum in London during the 19th century, with the development of exchange-traded options on government bonds.

20th Century: Institutionalization and Innovation

The 20th century witnessed remarkable advancements in options markets, driven by financial innovation and the growing need for risk management:

1. **Options Clearing Corporation (OCC)**: In 1973, the Options Clearing Corporation was founded to facilitate the clearing and settlement of options contracts, enhancing market safety and efficiency.

2. **Black-Scholes-Merton Model**: The introduction of the Black-Scholes-Merton option pricing model in 1973 revolutionized options markets. This model provided a theoretical framework for valuing options and understanding their pricing dynamics.

3. **Listed Options**: The establishment of organized exchanges for trading standardized listed options, such as the Chicago Board Options Exchange (CBOE), marked a significant milestone in options market development.

21st Century: Diverse Products and Global Markets

In the 21st century, options markets have expanded into a global arena, offering an array of products beyond traditional equity options:

1. **Exchange-Traded Funds (ETFs)**: The rise of ETFs has led to the development of options on ETF shares, allowing investors to hedge or speculate on the performance of entire sectors and asset classes.

2. **Volatility Products**: The advent of volatility-linked products, such as VIX futures and options, has provided new opportunities for traders to manage and speculate on market volatility.

3. **Currency and Interest Rate Options**: Options markets have expanded to include currency options, interest rate options, and a wide range of derivatives tailored to meet the needs of institutions and investors worldwide.

This historical journey through the development of options markets underscores their enduring significance in modern finance. Options have evolved from ancient practices to sophisticated instruments traded on global exchanges, serving diverse purposes, from risk management to speculation. As we progress through this book, we will delve deeper into the mechanics, strategies, and contemporary applications of options in the ever-evolving world of finance.

Types of Options (American vs. European)

Options markets are diverse, offering a range of contract types to cater to the specific needs of investors and traders. Two primary categories of options contracts, American options and European options, stand out due to their distinct exercise features and implications for trading strategies. In this section, we delve into the characteristics and key differences between American and European options, providing a foundation for understanding these essential components of the options landscape.

American Options: Flexibility and Early Exercise

Characteristics of American Options:

1. **Early Exercise**: The defining feature of American options is their flexibility regarding exercise. Holders of American options have the right to exercise the option at any time before or on the expiration date. This feature grants investors the ability to seize profit opportunities or manage risk by exercising the option early.

2. **Wide Range of Underlyings**: American options are available on a wide range of underlying assets, including stocks, commodities, and indices. They are highly versatile and adaptable to various investment strategies.

3. **Commonly Traded**: American options are frequently traded in markets worldwide. They are widely available and liquid, making them a preferred choice for many investors.

Implications and Strategies for American Options:

1. **Strategic Flexibility**: The early exercise feature of American options provides strategic flexibility. Investors can choose to exercise the option when it is most advantageous, depending on market conditions and their investment objectives.

2. **Risk Management**: American options can be valuable tools for risk management. Investors can use them to hedge positions or protect gains by exercising the option early in the event of adverse price movements.

3. **Income Generation**: Traders often write (sell) American options to generate income. By selling these options, they receive premiums from buyers and may avoid early exercise if the option remains out of the money.

European Options: Precision and Simplicity

Characteristics of European Options:

1. **No Early Exercise**: European options differ from their American counterparts in that they do not allow early exercise. Holders of European options can only exercise the option at expiration. This feature simplifies the decision-making process for option holders.

2. **Common in European Markets**: European options are prevalent in European markets and exchanges. They are commonly used for various purposes, including equity and index options.

3. **Precision in Pricing**: European options are often favored in theoretical pricing models due to their clear-cut exercise rules. This precision simplifies the calculation of option prices and related financial derivatives.

Implications and Strategies for European Options:

1. **Reduced Complexity**: The absence of early exercise in European options reduces complexity for option holders. They do not need to continually assess whether early exercise is advantageous.

2. **Pricing Models**: European options are commonly used in pricing models like the Black-Scholes-Merton model due to their clear exercise rules. This model assumes that options can only be exercised at expiration, aligning with the European option structure.

3. **Strategic Planning**: Investors in European options must focus on strategic planning within the context of the expiration date. They may use these options for targeted investment or speculation on specific market movements.

Key Considerations and Choice of Options:

The choice between American and European options depends on individual investment objectives, market conditions, and trading strategies. Key considerations include:

◈ **Exercise Flexibility**: American options provide flexibility with early exercise, making them suitable for dynamic strategies and risk management.

◈ **Simplicity**: European options offer simplicity and precision in pricing but do not allow early exercise.

◈ **Market Liquidity**: Consider the liquidity of the specific options market for your chosen type of option, as it can impact trading costs and efficiency.

As we navigate through the complexities of options in subsequent chapters, it's crucial to bear in mind the distinct characteristics of American and European options. These features will play a vital role in shaping your approach to options trading and investment strategies, allowing you to tailor your actions to specific market conditions and objectives.

Option Payoff Diagrams

Understanding option payoff diagrams is fundamental to grasping the potential outcomes and risks associated with options trading strategies. These diagrams provide visual representations of how an option's profitability evolves in relation to the price of the underlying asset at expiration. In this section, we delve into the significance of option payoff diagrams, how to interpret them, and their practical application in decision-making.

The Basics of Option Payoff Diagrams:

1. **Horizontal Axis (Underlying Asset Price)**: The horizontal axis of the payoff diagram represents the possible prices of the underlying asset at expiration.

2. **Vertical Axis (Profit or Loss)**: The vertical axis depicts the profit or loss resulting from the option position at expiration.

3. **Breakeven Points**: Payoff diagrams highlight breakeven points where the option position transitions from a profit to a loss or vice versa. These points are where the option premium paid equals the profit or loss.

Interpreting Option Payoff Diagrams:

Long Call Option Payoff Diagram:

◈ The payoff diagram for a long call option is characterized by a limited loss (the premium paid) and unlimited profit potential.

◈ It shows a rising line, indicating that as the price of the underlying asset increases, the profit for the long call holder also increases.

◈ The breakeven point is the strike price plus the premium paid for the call option.

Short Call Option Payoff Diagram:

◈ The payoff diagram for a short call option displays a limited profit (the premium received) and unlimited loss potential.

◈ It exhibits a descending line, signifying that as the underlying asset's price rises, the loss for the short call writer increases.

◈ The breakeven point is the strike price plus the premium received for writing the call option.

Long Put Option Payoff Diagram:

◈ A long put option payoff diagram shows limited loss (the premium paid) and profit potential.

◈ It displays a descending line, indicating that as the underlying asset's price falls, the profit for the long put holder rises.

◈ The breakeven point is the strike price minus the premium paid for the put option.

Short Put Option Payoff Diagram:

◈ The payoff diagram for a short put option exhibits limited profit (the premium received) and limited loss potential.

◈ It shows a rising line, signifying that as the underlying asset's price declines, the loss for the short put writer increases.

◈ The breakeven point is the strike price minus the premium received for writing the put option.

Applications of Option Payoff Diagrams:

1. **Strategy Evaluation**: Traders and investors use payoff diagrams to assess the potential outcomes of specific options trading strategies. By visualizing how changes in the underlying asset's price impact profits and losses, they can make informed decisions.

2. **Risk Management**: Payoff diagrams aid in understanding and managing the risk associated with options positions. They help identify breakeven points and potential maximum losses.

3. **Hedging**: Option payoff diagrams assist in constructing hedging strategies to protect existing positions. For instance, an investor with a long stock position can use put options to create a protective put strategy, limiting potential losses.

4. **Speculation and Income Generation**: Traders can utilize payoff diagrams to design strategies for speculative purposes, aiming to profit from anticipated price movements. Additionally, options strategies like covered calls can generate income, and payoff diagrams facilitate their evaluation.

5. **Portfolio Diversification**: Payoff diagrams aid in assessing how options fit into a diversified portfolio. They provide insights into how options can impact overall portfolio risk and returns.

In summary, option payoff diagrams serve as invaluable tools for comprehending the risk and reward profiles of various options positions. They offer visual clarity, allowing traders and investors to make informed decisions and construct strategies tailored to their objectives and market expectations. As we explore the intricacies of options in subsequent chapters, the ability to interpret and apply these diagrams will be a cornerstone of effective options trading.

Option Pricing Factors (Underlying Price, Strike Price, Time to Expiry, Volatility, Interest Rate)

The pricing of options is a complex process influenced by several key factors. These factors collectively determine the fair market value of an option and play a crucial role in formulating options trading strategies. In this section, we explore the five primary factors that influence option pricing: underlying price, strike price, time to expiry, volatility, and interest rates.

1. Underlying Price:

The price of the underlying asset, such as a stock, commodity, or index, is a fundamental determinant of option pricing.

◈ **Call Options**: As the underlying price rises, the value of call options generally increases. Call options give the holder the right to buy the underlying asset, so they become more valuable when the asset's price is higher than the strike price.

◈ **Put Options**: Conversely, put options tend to increase in value as the underlying price falls. Put options give the holder the right to sell the underlying asset, and they become more valuable when the asset's price is lower than the strike price.

2. Strike Price:

The strike price, also known as the exercise price, is the pre-determined price at which the option holder can buy (for call options) or sell (for put options) the underlying asset.

◈ **Call Options**: When the strike price is lower, call options tend to have higher value, as they allow the holder to buy the asset at a lower price.

◈ **Put Options**: Conversely, for put options, a higher strike price typically results in higher option value, as it allows the holder to sell the asset at a higher price.

3. Time to Expiry:

The time remaining until the option's expiration date is a critical factor in option pricing.

◈ **Call and Put Options**: Options with more time to expiry tend to have higher premiums because they offer the holder a longer window of opportunity for the underlying asset's price to move in a favorable direction.

◈ **Time Decay**: As an option approaches its expiration date, its time value diminishes, contributing to time decay, which can erode the option's value, especially in the final weeks or days leading up to expiration.

4. Volatility:

Volatility measures the degree of price fluctuations in the underlying asset. Higher volatility generally leads to higher option premiums.

◈ **Call and Put Options**: Options on highly volatile assets are more valuable because there is a greater likelihood of substantial price movements, potentially resulting in profits for the option holder.

5. Interest Rate:

Interest rates influence option pricing, primarily through their impact on the cost of carrying the underlying asset and the time value of money.

◈ **Call Options**: Higher interest rates tend to increase the value of call options because they raise the cost of holding the underlying asset, making it more expensive to wait and buy it later.

◈ **Put Options**: Conversely, higher interest rates may decrease the value of put options as they increase the cost of maintaining short positions.

Option Pricing Models:

To calculate option prices accurately, financial models like the Black-Scholes-Merton model and the Binomial model are often employed. These models incorporate the five pricing factors mentioned above, along with other variables, to provide estimates of option prices.

Understanding these pricing factors and their interplay is essential for options traders and investors. It allows them to assess the fair value of options, create strategies that align with their market expectations, and manage risk effectively. Throughout this book, we will explore how these factors come into play in various options trading strategies, providing practical insights into the dynamic world of options trading.

Chapter 2: Option Pricing Models

Black-Scholes-Merton Model

The Black-Scholes-Merton model is a foundational mathematical tool in the world of finance, particularly in the valuation of options. Developed by economists Fischer Black and Myron Scholes in 1973, with further contributions by Robert Merton, this model revolutionized options pricing by providing a formula to calculate the theoretical price of European-style options. In this chapter, we will delve into the workings of the Black-Scholes-Merton model, its assumptions, and its practical applications.

Assumptions of the Black-Scholes-Merton Model:

1. **Constant Volatility**: The model assumes that volatility remains constant over the option's life, a characteristic particularly applicable to European options.

2. **Efficient Markets**: The model presumes that markets are efficient, meaning no arbitrage opportunities exist, and prices follow a random walk.

3. **Constant Risk-Free Interest Rate**: The model assumes a constant risk-free interest rate over the option's life.

4. **No Dividends**: The Black-Scholes-Merton model assumes that the underlying asset does not pay any dividends during the option's life.

5. **Log-Normally Distributed Returns**: It assumes that the returns of the underlying asset are log-normally distributed, meaning they follow a specific statistical distribution.

Interpreting the Formula:

◈ The formula calculates the present value of the expected payoff of the option at expiration based on risk-neutral probabilities.

◈ It considers the difference between the current price of the underlying asset and the strike price.

◈ Volatility, time to expiration, interest rate, and dividend yield all play critical roles in determining the option price.

Practical Applications:

1. **Pricing Options**: The Black-Scholes-Merton model is extensively used by options traders and market makers to calculate the theoretical prices of options, enabling them to make informed trading decisions.

2. **Risk Management**: Traders utilize the model to assess the risk associated with their options positions and design hedging strategies to mitigate risk exposure.

3. **Strategy Formulation**: Investors use the model to create and optimize options trading strategies based on their market expectations and risk tolerance.

4. **Academic Research and Analysis**: The Black-Scholes-Merton model forms the basis for much of the academic research and analysis in options pricing and related fields.

The Black-Scholes-Merton model has significantly influenced the world of finance by providing a framework for pricing options and understanding their dynamics. While it has its limitations and assumptions that may not always hold true in real markets, it remains a foundational tool for options traders and academics alike, providing valuable insights into option pricing and risk assessment. In the subsequent chapters, we will explore other important option pricing models and their practical applications in detail.

Binomial Option Pricing Model

The Binomial Option Pricing Model is a versatile and widely used method for valuing options, particularly in situations where the assumptions of the Black-Scholes-Merton model are not met. Developed by economists Cox, Ross, and Rubinstein in the early 1970s, this model offers a more flexible approach to pricing options by discretizing time into small intervals and modeling the underlying asset's price movements as a series of binary (up or down) movements. In this chapter, we will explore the principles, assumptions, and practical applications of the Binomial Option Pricing Model.

Key Components and Assumptions:

1. **Time Discretization**: The Binomial Model divides the option's time to expiration into discrete time steps, often denoted as Δt, allowing for more precise modeling of complex situations.

2. **Up and Down Movements**: During each time step, the underlying asset's price can either move up by a factor of u or down by a factor of d. These factors represent the expected return and volatility of the asset.

3. **Risk-Neutral Pricing**: Similar to the Black-Scholes-Merton model, the Binomial Model assumes that markets are efficient, and pricing should be done in a risk-neutral framework. This implies that the expected return on the underlying asset equals the risk-free rate.

Practical Applications:

1. **Versatility**: The Binomial Model is flexible and can accommodate various assumptions, making it suitable for valuing options in situations where the Black-Scholes-Merton model's assumptions do not hold.

2. **American Options**: Unlike the Black-Scholes-Merton model, the Binomial Model can value American-style options, which can be exercised before expiration. It does this by comparing the option's value if exercised immediately to its value if held until expiration at each step.

3. **Complex Dividend Structures**: It can handle complex dividend structures, including irregular dividend payments during the option's life.

4. **Risk Management**: Traders and investors use the Binomial Model to assess and manage the risk associated with options positions and construct hedging strategies.

5. **Education and Understanding**: The Binomial Model is often used in educational settings to teach the fundamental concepts of option pricing and risk-neutral probabilities.

In summary, the Binomial Option Pricing Model is a versatile and valuable tool for valuing options in a variety of scenarios. Its ability to accommodate different assumptions and handle American-style options makes it particularly useful in practice. Traders and investors often turn to this model when faced with complex situations or when the assumptions of the Black-Scholes-Merton model are not met. As we progress through this book, we will explore additional option pricing models and their applications in greater detail.

The Greeks (Delta, Gamma, Theta, Vega, Rho)

In options trading, understanding the Greeks is essential. The Greeks are a set of risk measures that quantify how sensitive the price of an option is to various factors. They provide valuable insights into how an option's value changes in response to changes in the underlying asset's price, volatility, time to expiration, interest rates, and dividend yields. In this chapter, we will explore the five primary Greeks: Delta, Gamma, Theta, Vega, and Rho.

1. Delta (Δ):

Delta measures the sensitivity of an option's price to changes in the price of the underlying asset. It represents the change in the option price for a $1 change in the underlying asset's price.

◈ **Call Options**: Delta for call options ranges from 0 to 1. A call option with a delta of 0.6, for example, implies that for every $1 increase in the underlying asset's price, the call option's price will increase by $0.60.

◈ **Put Options**: Delta for put options ranges from -1 to 0. A put option with a delta of -0.4 indicates that for every $1 increase in the underlying asset's price, the put option's price will decrease by $0.40.

Delta also provides insights into the probability of an option expiring in the money. For example, a call option with a delta of 0.70 suggests a 70% chance of expiring in the money.

2. Gamma (Γ):

Gamma measures the rate of change of an option's delta in response to changes in the underlying asset's price. It represents how much delta will change for a $1 move in the underlying asset's price.

◈ Gamma is highest for at-the-money options and decreases as options move further in or out of the money.

◈ It quantifies the curvature of the option price graph, indicating how delta may change as the underlying asset's price changes.

3. Theta (Θ):

Theta measures the rate of time decay in an option's price. It represents the change in the option price for a one-day decrease in the time to expiration.

◈ Theta is typically negative for both call and put options, as options lose value as they approach expiration.

◈ It highlights the cost of holding an option position and encourages traders to consider time decay when formulating strategies.

4. Vega (ν):

Vega measures the sensitivity of an option's price to changes in implied volatility. It represents the change in the option price for a 1% increase in implied volatility.

◈ Higher Vega values indicate that an option's price is more sensitive to changes in volatility.

◈ Vega is particularly crucial for traders seeking to capitalize on changes in market volatility.

5. Rho (ρ):

Rho measures the sensitivity of an option's price to changes in interest rates. It represents the change in the option price for a 1% change in the risk-free interest rate.

◈ For call options, Rho is positive, meaning call option prices generally increase with rising interest rates.

◈ For put options, Rho is negative, indicating that put option prices tend to decrease as interest rates rise.

Practical Applications:

1. **Risk Management**: Traders use the Greeks to assess and manage the risk associated with their options positions. By understanding how changes in factors like underlying price, volatility, and time impact their positions, they can make informed decisions.

2. **Strategy Formulation**: The Greeks are integral to strategy formulation. Traders design options strategies based on their outlook for these factors and how they will affect their positions.

3. **Hedging**: Hedging strategies often involve adjusting options positions to offset changes in the Greeks. For example, delta-hedging involves adjusting the position to maintain a neutral delta.

4. **Position Sizing**: Understanding the Greeks helps traders determine the appropriate size of their options positions relative to their risk tolerance and market expectations.

In summary, the Greeks are essential tools for options traders and investors. They provide valuable insights into the risk and sensitivity of options positions to changes in underlying factors. By monitoring and managing the Greeks, traders can make more informed decisions and develop strategies that align with their objectives and market views.

Implied Volatility and Option Pricing

Implied volatility is a critical concept in options trading and pricing. It represents the market's expectations for future volatility of the underlying asset and plays a significant role in determining option prices. In this chapter, we will explore the concept of implied volatility, its calculation, and its impact on option pricing.

Understanding Implied Volatility:

1. **Historical vs. Implied Volatility**: Historical volatility is a measure of past price fluctuations in the underlying asset, while implied volatility reflects the expected future volatility implied by the option's market price.

2. **Options Pricing Models**: Implied volatility is an input in many options pricing models, including the Black-Scholes-Merton model

and the Binomial Model. In these models, implied volatility helps estimate the future potential price range of the underlying asset.

Calculation of Implied Volatility:

Implied volatility cannot be directly observed in the market. Instead, it is backward-calculated using option prices and options pricing models. The process involves iteratively adjusting the implied volatility until the calculated option price matches the market price. This backward calculation is often done using numerical methods, and various software tools are available for this purpose.

Impact on Option Pricing:

Implied volatility has a direct and significant impact on option prices. Here's how it affects call and put option prices:

1. **Call Options**:

◈ Higher implied volatility increases the prices of call options. This is because a higher expected future volatility suggests a greater chance of the underlying asset rising significantly in value, potentially resulting in higher profits for call option holders.

2. **Put Options**:

◈ Like call options, higher implied volatility leads to higher put option prices. Increased expected future volatility implies a greater chance of the underlying asset experiencing substantial declines, making put options more valuable as a means of protection.

Practical Considerations:

1. **Volatility Skew**: Implied volatility is not uniform across all strike prices and expiration dates. The volatility skew or smile refers to the variation in implied volatility with respect to different strikes and

maturities. It is a result of market participants' differing views on future price movements.

2. **Earnings Announcements and Events**: Implied volatility tends to increase before significant events like earnings announcements, product launches, or economic reports. Traders often refer to this as "event-driven volatility."

3. **Implied Volatility as an Indicator**: Some traders use implied volatility as a market sentiment indicator. High implied volatility may suggest uncertainty or potential market turbulence, while low implied volatility can indicate calm and stability.

Trading Strategies and Implied Volatility:

1. **Volatility Trading**: Some traders specialize in trading volatility itself, using strategies like straddles and strangles to profit from expected increases in implied volatility.

2. **Volatility Contraction**: Conversely, traders may take positions that profit from a decrease in implied volatility. This is common after significant events when implied volatility tends to revert to lower levels.

3. **Earnings Plays**: Traders often employ options strategies around earnings announcements, capitalizing on changes in implied volatility before and after the event.

In conclusion, implied volatility is a crucial component of options pricing and trading. Understanding the concept and its impact on option prices is essential for options traders and investors. Implied volatility reflects market expectations and can offer insights into the market's perception of future price movements. By incorporating implied volatility into their strategies, traders can make more informed decisions and adapt to changing market conditions.

Limitations of Option Pricing Models

Option pricing models, such as the Black-Scholes-Merton model and the Binomial model, provide valuable frameworks for estimating option prices and understanding their dynamics. However, it's essential to recognize their limitations and constraints. In this chapter, we will explore the key limitations of option pricing models.

1. Assumptions May Not Reflect Reality:

◈ Most option pricing models rely on simplifying assumptions that may not hold in real financial markets. For example, assumptions of constant volatility, risk-free interest rates, and efficient markets may not accurately represent market conditions.

2. Constant Volatility Assumption:

◈ The assumption of constant volatility is a significant limitation. In reality, volatility can change over time, sometimes abruptly, which can result in significant discrepancies between model estimates and market prices.

3. No Consideration of Dividends:

◈ Many option pricing models do not account for dividends paid by the underlying asset. This can be a substantial limitation for options on stocks that pay dividends, as dividends can affect option prices significantly.

4. Lack of Jump Risk Modeling:

◈ Option pricing models typically assume continuous price movements, ignoring the possibility of sudden jumps in the underlying asset's price. In volatile markets or during major news events, these jumps can occur and lead to pricing inaccuracies.

5. American vs. European Options:

◈ The Black-Scholes-Merton model is designed primarily for European-style options, which can only be exercised at expiration. It may not accurately value American-style options, which can be exercised at any time before expiration.

6. Market Frictions:

◈ Real financial markets involve transaction costs, taxes, and other frictions that are not considered in most option pricing models. These frictions can impact the profitability of options strategies.

7. Incomplete Information:

◈ Models often rely on publicly available information, which may not capture all relevant market dynamics and information asymmetries.

8. Complex Securities:

◈ Some option pricing models may struggle to accurately value complex securities, such as exotic options or structured products with non-standard features.

9. Limited in Market Crises:

◈ Option pricing models may struggle to capture extreme market conditions and rare events, such as market crashes or financial crises. These events can lead to significant discrepancies between model prices and market prices.

10. No Accounting for Behavioral Factors: - Models typically assume rational behavior and do not account for behavioral factors, which can drive market movements and option pricing.

11. Overreliance on Historical Data: - Models that use historical data for inputs may not account for changes in market dynamics or regimes, leading to inaccurate pricing during market shifts.

12. Lack of Flexibility: - Some models, while powerful, may lack the flexibility to adapt to various real-world scenarios and may not capture complex market dynamics accurately.

Practical Considerations:

◈ Traders and investors should use option pricing models as tools for estimation rather than as definitive pricing mechanisms. Real-world market conditions often deviate from model assumptions.

◈ Risk management and an awareness of model limitations are crucial. Traders should incorporate a margin of safety in their strategies to account for potential pricing discrepancies.

◈ In some cases, traders may rely on more sophisticated models or proprietary pricing algorithms to better align with market realities.

In summary, option pricing models are valuable tools for estimating option prices and understanding their sensitivities to various factors. However, they have limitations that traders and investors must be aware of when using them in real-world decision-making. Flexibility, adaptability, and a critical assessment of model outputs are key to effectively navigating these limitations in options trading and investment.

Chapter 3: Volatility Basics

Understanding Volatility

Volatility is a fundamental concept in financial markets, and it plays a crucial role in options trading and pricing. In this chapter, we will explore the concept of volatility, its measurement, and its significance in the context of options trading.

What Is Volatility?

Volatility refers to the degree of variation or fluctuation in the price of an asset over time. It quantifies the degree of uncertainty or risk associated with an asset's price movement. In financial markets, volatility is typically expressed as a percentage and is often synonymous with market risk.

Types of Volatility:

1. **Historical Volatility**: This measures the past price fluctuations of an asset. It is calculated by analyzing historical price data. Historical volatility provides insights into how volatile an asset has been in the past.

2. **Implied Volatility**: Implied volatility reflects the market's expectations for future price fluctuations. It is derived from option prices and represents the consensus view of market participants regarding future volatility. Implied volatility is a critical component of options pricing.

The Importance of Volatility in Options Trading:

Volatility is of paramount importance in options trading for several reasons:

1. **Impact on Option Prices**: Higher volatility tends to lead to higher option prices. Options become more valuable when there is a greater potential for significant price movements in the underlying asset.

2. **Risk Assessment**: Volatility is a key factor in assessing the risk associated with options positions. Traders use volatility measures to understand how sensitive their positions are to price fluctuations.

3. **Strategy Selection**: Traders often select options strategies based on their outlook for volatility. For instance, in high-volatility environments, strategies like straddles and strangles may be employed to profit from expected price swings.

4. **Hedging**: Volatility can influence hedging decisions. Traders may adjust their positions to hedge against adverse price movements when they anticipate increased volatility.

Measuring Volatility:

Several methods are used to measure volatility:

1. **Standard Deviation**: This statistical measure quantifies the degree of variation in historical price data. A higher standard deviation indicates greater volatility.

2. **Historical Volatility**: Calculated as the standard deviation of past price returns over a specified period. It provides a historical perspective on volatility.

3. **Implied Volatility**: Derived from option prices using options pricing models like the Black-Scholes-Merton model or the Binomial model. Implied volatility represents the market's forward-looking expectation of volatility.

Volatility Index (VIX):

The CBOE Volatility Index, known as the VIX, is often referred to as the "fear gauge" or "fear index." It measures implied volatility in the S&P 500 index options market. The VIX provides insights into market sentiment, with higher values suggesting increased expected volatility and potentially heightened uncertainty.

Factors Influencing Volatility:

Several factors can impact volatility in financial markets:

1. **Economic Events**: Economic data releases, corporate earnings reports, and geopolitical events can trigger significant price swings and changes in volatility.

2. **Market Sentiment**: Investor sentiment and perceptions of risk can drive volatility. Fear and uncertainty can lead to heightened volatility, while complacency can result in lower volatility.

3. **Liquidity**: Markets with low liquidity are often more susceptible to sharp price movements and increased volatility.

4. **News and Events**: Unexpected news events, such as natural disasters or geopolitical crises, can have a profound impact on volatility.

Volatility and Options Trading Strategies:

Traders use volatility-based strategies to adapt to changing market conditions. Some common strategies include:

1. **Straddle**: Involves buying both a call and a put option with the same strike price and expiration date, anticipating a significant price move.

2. **Strangle**: Similar to a straddle, but the call and put options have different strike prices. It's used when the trader expects price movement but is uncertain about the direction.

3. **Iron Condor**: Combines call and put credit spreads to profit from low volatility and stable price movements.

4. **Calendar Spread**: Involves buying and selling options with different expiration dates to capitalize on changes in implied volatility.

In summary, volatility is a central concept in options trading. It quantifies price fluctuations and plays a pivotal role in option pricing, risk assessment, and strategy selection. Understanding volatility and its dynamics is essential for options traders, as it allows them to make informed decisions in an ever-changing financial landscape.

Historical vs. Implied Volatility

Volatility is a key factor in options trading, and understanding the differences between historical and implied volatility is essential for traders and investors. In this chapter, we will explore the distinctions between these two types of volatility and their significance in the world of options.

Historical Volatility:

Definition: Historical volatility measures the past price fluctuations of an asset over a specific period. It provides insights into how volatile an asset has been historically.

Calculation: To calculate historical volatility, follow these steps:

1. Select a historical price data set, such as daily closing prices for a stock.

2. Calculate the daily returns by taking the percentage change in price from one day to the next.

3. Compute the standard deviation of these daily returns over a specified time frame, typically annualized.

Characteristics and Significance:

◈ Historical volatility is backward-looking, reflecting past market conditions.

◈ It provides traders with a sense of how an asset has behaved in the past, which can help assess risk and formulate trading strategies.

◈ High historical volatility suggests that an asset has experienced substantial price swings, while low historical volatility indicates more stable price movements.

Implied Volatility:

Definition: Implied volatility reflects the market's expectations for future price fluctuations of an asset. It is derived from option prices and represents the consensus view of market participants regarding future volatility.

Calculation: Implied volatility cannot be directly observed but is backward-calculated using option prices and options pricing models, such as the Black-Scholes-Merton model. Traders use numerical methods to estimate implied volatility that would make the model's output match the current market option prices.

Characteristics and Significance:

◈ Implied volatility is forward-looking, capturing market expectations.

◈ It is a critical component in options pricing models, such as the Black-Scholes-Merton model, and significantly influences option prices.

◈ Implied volatility can vary among different options with the same underlying asset, strike price, and expiration date, indicating market participants' differing views on future price movements.

Key Differences:

1. **Direction:** Historical volatility looks back at past price movements, while implied volatility looks forward to anticipate future price swings.

2. **Use:** Traders use historical volatility primarily for risk assessment and strategy formulation based on past data. Implied volatility is used for options pricing and assessing market expectations.

3. **Calculation:** Historical volatility is calculated from past price data, while implied volatility is calculated backward using option prices and pricing models.

4. **Interpretation:** High historical volatility suggests past price swings, while high implied volatility suggests market expectations of future price uncertainty.

5. **Influence on Options Prices:** Implied volatility directly affects option prices, while historical volatility does not impact option values directly.

Practical Applications:

◈ Traders often compare implied volatility to historical volatility to identify discrepancies that may present trading opportunities. For example, if implied volatility is significantly higher than historical volatility, it may signal overpriced options.

◈ Implied volatility is a key component in options trading strategies. Traders may seek to buy options with relatively low implied volatility and sell options with relatively high implied volatility, aiming to profit from changes in implied volatility.

In conclusion, historical and implied volatility serve different purposes in options trading. Historical volatility provides insights into past price behavior, while implied volatility reflects market expectations of future price movements. Both are essential tools for traders and investors, enabling them to make informed decisions in the dynamic world of options.

Volatility as a Measure of Risk

Volatility is a crucial measure of risk in financial markets, and it plays a central role in options trading and investment decisions. In this chapter, we will delve into the concept of volatility as a measure of risk and its significance in assessing and managing risk in various financial instruments, with a particular focus on options.

Volatility as Risk:

1. **Definition**: Volatility represents the degree of variation in the price of an asset over time. As a measure of risk, it quantifies the uncertainty and potential for price fluctuations associated with an investment.

2. **Asset Classes**: Volatility is a universal concept that applies to various asset classes, including stocks, bonds, commodities, and currencies. Different financial instruments exhibit varying levels of volatility.

Significance in Risk Assessment:

Volatility is essential for risk assessment and risk management in several ways:

1. **Risk Identification**: Higher volatility often indicates a riskier asset or investment. Assets with greater price swings are inherently riskier because they can lead to substantial gains or losses.

2. **Portfolio Diversification**: Volatility is a critical consideration when constructing diversified portfolios. Investors aim to balance assets with different levels of volatility to manage overall portfolio risk.

3. **Risk Tolerance**: Understanding volatility helps investors assess their risk tolerance. An investor with a low tolerance for large price swings may prefer less volatile assets.

4. **Risk-Return Trade-off**: Volatility is closely linked to the risk-return trade-off. In general, riskier assets with higher volatility offer the potential for greater returns but also come with increased risk.

Volatility in Options Trading:

Volatility plays a unique and pivotal role in options trading:

1. **Options Pricing**: Volatility is a fundamental component in options pricing models, such as the Black-Scholes-Merton model. Higher volatility leads to higher option premiums, as it indicates a greater potential for price movements.

2. **Risk Assessment**: Traders use volatility measures to assess the risk associated with their options positions. Understanding how options prices are influenced by volatility helps in managing risk exposure.

3. **Strategy Selection**: Volatility outlook influences strategy selection. Traders may adopt different strategies depending on whether they anticipate low, moderate, or high volatility.

4. **Hedging**: Volatility can drive the need for hedging strategies. Traders may adjust their options positions to mitigate risk in response to changing volatility conditions.

Volatility Index (VIX):

The CBOE Volatility Index (VIX), often referred to as the "fear gauge," measures expected volatility in the S&P 500 index options market. The VIX is widely used as an indicator of market sentiment and risk appetite. Higher VIX values typically indicate increased expected market volatility and uncertainty.

Managing Risk with Volatility:

1. **Diversification**: Diversifying a portfolio across different asset classes and regions can help reduce risk by mitigating the impact of volatility in a single asset or market.

2. **Risk-Adjusted Returns**: Investors often assess investments not just based on their potential returns but on the risk-adjusted returns. Investments with higher returns should be evaluated in the context of their associated volatility.

3. **Stop Loss Orders**: Traders may use stop loss orders to limit losses in volatile markets. These orders automatically trigger a sale when an asset's price reaches a predetermined level.

4. **Options Strategies**: Traders can employ options strategies like straddles or collars to protect against or profit from changes in volatility.

In conclusion, volatility serves as a critical measure of risk in financial markets. It informs risk assessment, portfolio construction, and trading strategies, particularly in options trading where it directly impacts pricing and risk management. By understanding and effectively navigating volatility, investors and traders can make informed decisions and manage risk in a dynamic and ever-changing financial landscape.

Volatility Smile and Skew

The volatility smile and skew are important concepts in options trading, particularly in understanding how implied volatility varies with strike prices. In this chapter, we will explore the volatility smile and skew, what they represent, and their significance in options markets.

Volatility Smile:

1. **Definition**: The volatility smile refers to the graphical shape of implied volatility as a function of strike prices for a given expiration date. In a volatility smile, the implied volatility tends to be higher for out-of-the-money (OTM) and in-the-money (ITM) options, with a minimum at or near the at-the-money (ATM) strike price.

2. **Interpretation**:

◈ A volatility smile implies that options with strike prices significantly above or below the current market price of the underlying asset are perceived to have a higher level of risk and, therefore, higher implied volatility.

◈ Options at or near the current market price are considered less risky and have lower implied volatility.

3. **Causes**:

◈ The volatility smile often arises due to market participants' belief that extreme price movements are more likely than what is predicted by the Black-Scholes-Merton model.

◈ It can also result from demand and supply dynamics in the options market, as traders may be willing to pay higher premiums for options that provide protection against extreme price events.

Volatility Skew:

1. **Definition**: The volatility skew is a more specific aspect of the volatility smile. It focuses on the shape of implied volatility concerning options of the same type (e.g., all call options or all put options) but with different strike prices. Specifically, it examines how implied volatility changes with strike price while keeping the expiration date constant.

2. **Types of Skew**:

◈ **Positive Skew**: This occurs when implied volatility increases as strike prices decrease, meaning that OTM put options have higher implied volatility than ATM or ITM put options. It is often associated with markets where there is greater concern about downside risk (e.g., equity markets).

◈ **Negative Skew**: In contrast, negative skew occurs when implied volatility rises as strike prices increase, leading to higher implied volatility for OTM call options than for ATM or ITM call options. This skew may be observed in markets where there is more concern about upside risk (e.g., foreign exchange markets).

3. **Significance**:

◈ The volatility skew reflects market sentiment about potential extreme price movements. Positive skew indicates more concern about downside risk, while negative skew suggests more concern about upside risk.

◈ Traders often use the skew to inform their options strategies. For example, in a market with a positive skew, a trader might consider buying OTM puts as a hedge against downside risk.

Practical Implications:

1. **Trading Strategies**: Understanding the volatility smile and skew can guide options traders in selecting strategies that align with market sentiment and risk outlook.

2. **Risk Management**: The skew can be a valuable tool for risk management, as it highlights options with higher implied volatility that may provide better protection during adverse market conditions.

3. **Structuring Trades**: Traders can structure trades that take advantage of the skew by buying options with relatively lower implied volatility and selling options with relatively higher implied volatility.

4. **Market Sentiment**: The presence and shape of the volatility smile and skew provide insights into market sentiment and can be used as indicators of expected market movements.

In summary, the volatility smile and skew are important components of options pricing and trading. They reflect market perceptions of risk and can guide traders in selecting strategies and managing risk exposure. By understanding these concepts, options market participants can make more informed decisions in a dynamic and ever-changing financial landscape.

Volatility Trading Strategies

Volatility trading strategies are approaches used by traders and investors to profit from changes in market volatility. These strategies are particularly relevant in the world of options trading, where volatility plays a pivotal role in determining option prices. In this chapter, we will explore various volatility trading strategies and their practical applications.

1. Volatility Spreads:

Definition: Volatility spreads involve simultaneously buying and selling options with different strike prices or expiration dates to take advantage of discrepancies in implied volatility levels.

Examples:

⟐ **Calendar Spreads**: In a calendar spread, a trader simultaneously sells an option with a shorter expiration date and buys an option with a longer expiration date. This strategy profits from changes in implied volatility between the two expiration dates.

◈ **Vertical Spreads**: Vertical spreads involve buying and selling options with the same expiration date but different strike prices. Depending on whether the trader buys a call and sells a higher strike call (bull call spread) or buys a put and sells a lower strike put (bear put spread), the strategy can profit from increasing or decreasing volatility, respectively.

2. Straddle and Strangle Strategies:

Definition: Straddle and strangle strategies involve buying both a call and a put option with the same expiration date but different strike prices. These strategies profit from significant price movements, regardless of whether they are up or down.

Examples:

◈ **Long Straddle**: A long straddle involves buying an at-the-money (ATM) call and an ATM put option simultaneously. It's used when the trader expects significant price movement but is uncertain about the direction.

◈ **Long Strangle**: Similar to a straddle, a long strangle involves buying an out-of-the-money (OTM) call and an OTM put option simultaneously. It profits from significant price swings but at a lower cost than a straddle.

3. Volatility ETFs and ETNs:

Definition: Exchange-traded funds (ETFs) and exchange-traded notes (ETNs) designed to track volatility indexes or indices can be used for volatility trading. These products provide exposure to changes in market volatility.

Examples:

◈ **VIX-Linked Products**: ETFs or ETNs linked to the CBOE Volatility Index (VIX) allow traders to take positions based on expected changes in market volatility.

4. Volatility Risk Reversals:

Definition: A volatility risk reversal strategy involves simultaneously selling an out-of-the-money (OTM) put option and buying an OTM call option (bullish risk reversal) or selling an OTM call option and buying an OTM put option (bearish risk reversal). These strategies can profit from shifts in market sentiment and volatility expectations.

Examples:

◈ **Bullish Risk Reversal**: A trader may sell an OTM put option and buy an OTM call option when they anticipate a bullish move and a potential increase in volatility.

◈ **Bearish Risk Reversal**: Conversely, a trader may sell an OTM call option and buy an OTM put option when they expect a bearish move and a rise in volatility.

5. Volatility Index Options:

Definition: Options on volatility indexes like the VIX can be used to trade changes in market volatility directly.

Examples:

◈ **VIX Options**: Traders can buy and sell options on the VIX, which allow them to speculate on changes in implied volatility.

Practical Considerations:

1. **Risk Management**: Volatility trading can be profitable but also involves risks. Traders should carefully manage position sizes and be prepared for unexpected market moves.

2. **Market Timing**: Timing is critical in volatility trading. Traders must anticipate changes in volatility and enter and exit positions accordingly.

3. **Comprehensive Analysis**: Successful volatility traders often rely on a combination of technical and fundamental analysis to inform their strategies.

4. **Options Knowledge**: Volatility trading strategies are closely tied to options trading. Traders should have a solid understanding of options and how they interact with volatility.

5. **Diversification**: As with any trading strategy, diversifying across multiple positions or strategies can help manage risk.

In summary, volatility trading strategies provide avenues for traders and investors to profit from changes in market volatility. These strategies can be used in various market conditions and offer flexibility in capturing potential opportunities arising from fluctuations in implied volatility levels. However, it's essential to approach volatility trading with a comprehensive understanding of options and risk management principles.

Chapter 4: Volatility Forecasting

Historical Volatility Calculation

Historical volatility is a key metric used in options trading and risk assessment. It quantifies the level of price variation in an asset over a specific historical period, offering insights into its past behavior, which can be used to forecast future price movements. Calculating historical volatility involves a series of steps:

1. **Data Collection**: Begin by gathering daily price data for the asset you're interested in analyzing. For example, when examining a stock, you'll typically collect the daily closing prices for that stock.

2. **Returns Calculation**: Calculate the daily returns for the asset. To do this, apply the following formula for each trading day within the historical period:

Daily Return=Today's Price−Yesterday's PriceYesterday's PriceDaily Return=Yesterday's PriceToday's Price−Yesterday's Price

This formula measures the percentage change in the asset's price from one day to the next. Repeat this calculation for each day in your historical dataset.

3. **Standard Deviation**: Once you have computed the daily returns, calculate the standard deviation of these returns. The standard deviation represents the average deviation of returns from their mean value and serves as the measure of historical volatility. To annualize this value, multiply it by the square root of the number of trading days in a year, typically 252 for stock markets:

Historical Volatility (Annualized)=Standard Deviation of Daily Returns×Number of Trading Days in a YearHistorical Volatility (Annualized)=Standard Deviation of Daily Returns×Number of Trading Days in a Year

The historical volatility, once calculated, can be expressed as a percentage and represents the asset's annualized volatility based on historical data.

Significance of Historical Volatility

Historical volatility holds significance in various aspects of options trading and risk assessment:

1. **Risk Evaluation**: It provides a quantifiable measure of an asset's historical price fluctuations, aiding traders and investors in assessing the potential risk associated with holding or trading that asset.

2. **Options Pricing**: Historical volatility serves as a critical input in options pricing models like the Black-Scholes-Merton model. It assists in estimating the fair value of options by indicating the probable range of future price movements.

3. **Strategy Selection**: Traders leverage historical volatility to choose appropriate options trading strategies that align with their risk tolerance and market expectations. Strategies may differ depending on whether historical volatility is high or low.

4. **Volatility Forecasting**: Historical volatility can also be employed as a foundation for forecasting future volatility. Traders often anticipate that an asset's future volatility will resemble its historical volatility patterns, aiding in strategy development.

In essence, historical volatility is a valuable metric in financial analysis, particularly in the context of options trading, as it facilitates risk assessment, pricing, strategy selection, and volatility forecasting based on past price behavior.

Implied Volatility Calculation

Implied volatility is a critical component in options pricing and trading. It reflects the market's expectations regarding future price fluctuations of an underlying asset. Unlike historical volatility, which is based on past price movements, implied volatility is forward-looking. In this chapter, we will explore how to calculate implied volatility and its significance in options trading.

Definition of Implied Volatility:

Implied volatility (IV) represents the market's consensus expectation of the future volatility of an underlying asset. It is derived from the prices of options on that asset and is a crucial input in options pricing models, such as the Black-Scholes-Merton model.

Calculating Implied Volatility:

Implied volatility cannot be directly observed but must be calculated using options pricing models and market prices of options with varying strike prices and expiration dates. The process involves iterative numerical methods, and traders often use specialized software or platforms for this calculation.

Here's a simplified outline of the steps to calculate implied volatility:

1. **Option Prices**: Gather market prices of options with different strike prices and the same expiration date for the underlying asset.

2. **Select an Options Pricing Model**: Choose an appropriate options pricing model, such as the Black-Scholes-Merton model or the Binomial model.

3. **Iterative Process**: Use numerical methods, such as the Newton-Raphson method, to iteratively adjust the implied volatility until the options pricing model's output closely matches the observed market prices of options.

4. **Implied Volatility Calculation**: The final value achieved for implied volatility through the iterative process represents the implied volatility for the selected options and expiration date.

Significance of Implied Volatility:

Implied volatility is of significant importance in options trading and risk assessment:

1. **Options Pricing**: Implied volatility directly influences the prices of options. Higher implied volatility leads to higher option premiums, as it indicates a greater expected range of future price movements.

2. **Market Sentiment**: Implied volatility provides insights into market sentiment and expectations. A rise in implied volatility often suggests increased uncertainty or anticipated price swings.

3. **Volatility Skew**: Implied volatility varies across different options with the same underlying asset but different strike prices. This volatility skew can offer valuable information about market perceptions of risk.

4. **Trading Strategies**: Traders use implied volatility to select appropriate trading strategies based on their outlook for future price volatility. For example, they may choose strategies that profit from expected changes in implied volatility.

5. **Risk Assessment**: Implied volatility helps traders assess the risk associated with specific options positions. It quantifies the level of uncertainty about future price movements.

In summary, implied volatility is a forward-looking measure of expected future price fluctuations derived from options market prices. It is a vital element in options pricing and trading, as it guides strategy selection, risk assessment, and market analysis. Calculating implied volatility involves iterative methods and specialized tools to match market option prices with options pricing models, ultimately providing valuable insights into market expectations.

GARCH Models for Volatility Forecasting

In the realm of financial analysis and forecasting, Generalized Autoregressive Conditional Heteroskedasticity (GARCH) models play a prominent role in estimating and predicting asset price volatility. In this chapter, we will delve into the concept of GARCH models, how they work, and their significance in volatility forecasting.

Definition of GARCH Models:

GARCH models are econometric models used to describe and forecast time series data with changing volatility over time. These models are particularly well-suited for capturing the volatility clustering phenomenon observed in financial markets, where periods of high volatility tend to cluster together.

Components of GARCH Models:

GARCH models typically consist of three key components:

1. **Autoregressive Component (AR)**: This component accounts for the lagged, or past, values of the squared returns (variance) of the asset's

price. It captures the persistence in volatility and adjusts for previous volatility levels.

2. **Moving Average Component (MA)**: The MA component involves lagged values of the past errors, or innovations, in the variance equation. It helps capture any short-term deviations from the long-term volatility trend.

3. **Conditional Heteroskedasticity (ARCH)**: The ARCH component models the conditional variance of the asset's returns, which varies based on past information, such as squared returns. It addresses the heteroskedasticity, or changing volatility, in the data.

GARCH(p, q) Model:

The notation GARCH(p, q) represents a GARCH model with p lags of the autoregressive component (AR) and q lags of the moving average component (MA). The specific choice of p and q depends on the characteristics of the financial data being analyzed.

How GARCH Models Work:

1. **Data Collection**: Gather historical time series data, typically daily returns or price data for the asset of interest.

2. **Model Specification**: Choose an appropriate GARCH model, such as GARCH(1,1) or GARCH(2,1), based on the observed characteristics of the data.

3. **Parameter Estimation**: Estimate the model parameters (p, q, and coefficients) using statistical methods like maximum likelihood estimation (MLE).

4. **Model Fitting**: Fit the GARCH model to the historical data to obtain the conditional variances and standardized residuals.

5. **Volatility Forecasting**: Use the estimated GARCH model to forecast future volatility. The model provides conditional variances, which can be used to predict the level of future price volatility.

Significance of GARCH Models in Volatility Forecasting:

GARCH models offer several advantages and practical applications in financial analysis:

1. **Volatility Forecasting**: GARCH models excel at forecasting future volatility levels, allowing traders and investors to make informed decisions about risk management and trading strategies.

2. **Risk Assessment**: By providing conditional volatility forecasts, GARCH models help assess the risk associated with specific asset positions or portfolios.

3. **Options Pricing**: GARCH-based volatility forecasts are used in options pricing models to estimate option premiums accurately.

4. **Portfolio Management**: Portfolio managers use GARCH models to optimize asset allocation and risk management within a portfolio.

5. **Risk Hedging**: GARCH forecasts enable hedging strategies that protect against adverse price movements during periods of heightened volatility.

In summary, GARCH models are powerful tools for forecasting volatility in financial markets. They are well-suited for capturing the changing nature of volatility over time and are widely employed in risk assessment, options pricing, and portfolio management. By providing insights into future volatility levels, GARCH models empower traders and investors to make informed decisions in a dynamic and uncertain financial landscape.

Option-Implied Volatility as a Forecasting Tool

Option-implied volatility, often referred to simply as implied volatility (IV), is a valuable tool in financial forecasting, particularly for predicting future asset price movements and market sentiment. In this chapter, we will explore how option-implied volatility works and its significance as a forecasting tool.

Definition of Implied Volatility:

Implied volatility (IV) represents the market's collective expectation of future price volatility for an underlying asset. It is derived from the prices of options on that asset and is an essential component in options pricing models, such as the Black-Scholes-Merton model.

How Option-Implied Volatility Works as a Forecasting Tool:

Option-implied volatility is a forward-looking measure that can be leveraged for various forecasting purposes:

1. **Expected Future Volatility**: IV provides a market consensus on the expected future volatility of an asset. High IV suggests an anticipated increase in price swings, while low IV indicates an expected decrease in volatility.

2. **Market Sentiment**: Changes in IV can indicate shifts in market sentiment. A sudden rise in IV may signal increased uncertainty or fear, while a decline in IV may suggest greater confidence or complacency.

3. **Event Anticipation**: IV often surges ahead of significant events such as earnings announcements, economic data releases, or geopolitical developments. Traders and investors can use IV as a leading indicator to anticipate market reactions to these events.

4. **Volatility Clusters**: Implied volatility tends to cluster during certain market conditions. For example, during market corrections or crises,

IV across various assets may simultaneously rise. Forecasting these volatility clusters can help prepare for turbulent market periods.

5. **Options Pricing and Risk Management**: IV directly impacts options prices. Traders can use IV to assess whether options are relatively expensive or inexpensive, guiding their options trading decisions and risk management strategies.

Using Implied Volatility for Forecasting:

1. **Volatility Regimes**: Analyze changes in IV to identify different volatility regimes in the market. Understanding these regimes can assist in adapting trading strategies to current market conditions.

2. **IV Skew and Term Structure**: Examining IV skew (variation in IV across different strike prices) and term structure (IV differences across various expiration dates) can provide insights into market expectations and potential price movements.

3. **Comparative Analysis**: Compare current IV levels to historical averages or benchmarks to gauge whether the market perceives the current environment as more or less volatile than usual.

4. **Volatility Surfaces**: Construct volatility surfaces that map IV across various strike prices and expirations. These surfaces can help visualize market expectations and inform trading decisions.

5. **Options Trading Strategies**: Incorporate IV analysis into options trading strategies. For example, a trader might sell options with high IV and buy options with relatively low IV, aiming to benefit from changes in IV.

6. **Risk Management**: Use IV as a risk management tool. Elevated IV can indicate potential risks, prompting traders to adjust their portfolios or implement protective strategies.

In conclusion, option-implied volatility serves as a versatile forecasting tool in finance. It offers insights into market expectations, sentiment, and potential future price movements. Traders and investors can leverage implied volatility to adapt their strategies, manage risk, and make informed decisions in a dynamic and uncertain financial landscape.

Volatility Term Structure and Surface

The volatility term structure and surface are important concepts in financial markets, particularly in the context of volatility forecasting, options pricing, and risk management. In this chapter, we will explore what the volatility term structure and surface represent and how they are used in forecasting and analysis.

Volatility Term Structure:

The volatility term structure, also known as the volatility curve or volatility smile (when plotted), provides insights into how implied volatility varies across different expiration dates for options on the same underlying asset. It reveals how market participants perceive future volatility for various time horizons. Key points regarding the volatility term structure include:

1. **Term Structure Shape**: The shape of the volatility term structure can vary. In typical scenarios, implied volatility tends to increase as the time to expiration increases, reflecting the market's expectation of greater uncertainty in the distant future. However, the shape can deviate from this pattern in response to specific events or market conditions.

2. **Inversion**: In some cases, the volatility term structure may invert, with shorter-term implied volatility exceeding longer-term implied volatility. This inversion can signal heightened near-term uncertainty or upcoming events that are expected to impact volatility.

3. **Volatility Clustering**: The term structure often exhibits volatility clustering, where implied volatility for nearby expirations tends to be more similar to each other compared to distant expirations. This phenomenon reflects the market's recognition that volatility tends to persist over certain time frames.

Volatility Surface:

The volatility surface extends the concept of the term structure by adding a dimension—the strike price of options. It illustrates how implied volatility varies across different expiration dates and strike prices for a specific underlying asset. Key points regarding the volatility surface include:

1. **Three-Dimensional Representation**: The volatility surface is typically visualized as a three-dimensional surface plot, with strike prices on one axis, expiration dates on another axis, and implied volatility values on the third axis. This representation provides a comprehensive view of market expectations.

2. **Volatility Smile and Skew**: The volatility surface often exhibits a smile or skew pattern. The smile refers to the upward or downward curvature of implied volatility for different strike prices at a specific expiration date. A skew represents the variation in implied volatility across different expiration dates for the same strike price.

3. **Options Pricing and Hedging**: The volatility surface is crucial in options pricing models, as it directly influences option premiums. Traders and risk managers use the surface to evaluate the pricing and hedging of options positions based on their specific strike prices and expirations.

Practical Applications:

1. **Options Pricing**: The volatility surface plays a central role in accurately pricing options. It accounts for variations in implied volatility across different strike prices and expirations, allowing for more precise valuation.

2. **Risk Management**: Understanding the term structure and surface helps in risk management, particularly in assessing the risk associated with options positions and portfolios under various market conditions.

3. **Volatility Forecasting**: Analysts and traders use the term structure and surface as inputs in forecasting future volatility, which is essential for making informed trading decisions.

4. **Strategy Selection**: The shape of the term structure and surface can influence the choice of options trading strategies. For example, traders may adopt strategies that exploit volatility skews or smile patterns.

In summary, the volatility term structure and surface provide critical insights into market expectations and the pricing of options. They are valuable tools for traders, analysts, and risk managers, helping them assess and forecast volatility, price options accurately, and make strategic decisions in response to market dynamics.

Chapter 5: Option Strategies for Income

Covered Call Writing

Covered call writing is a popular options strategy used by investors seeking to generate income from their existing stock holdings while potentially benefiting from limited price appreciation. In this chapter, we will explore covered call writing, how it works, its advantages, and its considerations in income generation.

Definition of Covered Call Writing:

A covered call, also known as a buy-write strategy, is executed when an investor who owns a specific amount of an underlying stock simultaneously sells (writes) call options on the same stock. The number of call options written is typically proportionate to the number of shares owned.

How Covered Call Writing Works:

Here's a step-by-step explanation of how covered call writing works:

1. **Stock Ownership**: The investor must own the underlying stock, typically in lots of 100 shares per options contract.

2. **Call Option Sale**: The investor sells call options on the stock they own. Each call option represents the right (but not the obligation) for the option buyer to purchase 100 shares of the underlying stock at a specified strike price before the option's expiration date.

3. **Expiration Date and Strike Price**: The investor selects an expiration date and strike price for the call options they sell. The strike price determines the price at which the stock will be sold if the call options are exercised.

4. **Premium Collection**: In exchange for selling the call options, the investor receives a premium (income). This premium is credited to their account immediately upon executing the covered call.

5. **Outcomes**:

◈ If the stock price remains below the call option's strike price until expiration, the call options expire worthless, and the investor keeps the premium as income.

◈ If the stock price rises above the call option's strike price, the options may be exercised, and the investor is obligated to sell their stock at the strike price. They still keep the premium received.

Advantages of Covered Call Writing:

1. **Income Generation**: The primary objective of covered call writing is to generate income from the premium received when selling call options.

2. **Enhanced Returns**: In addition to the premium income, investors may benefit from any modest price appreciation in the underlying stock.

3. **Reduced Cost Basis**: The premium income reduces the effective purchase price (cost basis) of the stock, providing some downside protection.

4. **Customizable Strategy**: Investors can tailor the strategy by choosing strike prices and expiration dates that align with their income goals and market expectations.

Considerations in Covered Call Writing:

1. **Limited Upside**: By selling call options, investors cap their potential profit at the strike price, missing out on significant price gains if the stock rallies.

2. **Obligation to Sell**: If the stock price surpasses the strike price, the investor is obligated to sell their shares at the strike price, potentially missing out on further price appreciation.

3. **Risk of Assignment**: Call options may be exercised at any time before expiration if they are in-the-money. Investors should be prepared for early assignment.

4. **Market Conditions**: Covered call writing is more effective in range-bound or slightly bullish markets. In strongly bullish markets, the strategy's profit potential is limited.

5. **Tax Implications**: Generating income through premiums may have tax consequences. Consult a tax advisor to understand the tax implications of covered call writing.

In conclusion, covered call writing is a versatile income-generating strategy that allows investors to earn premiums from their existing stock holdings while maintaining some participation in potential price gains. It offers advantages in terms of income generation and risk management but requires careful consideration of market conditions and trade-offs between income and upside potential.

Cash-Secured Put Writing

Cash-secured put writing is an options strategy employed by investors looking to generate income while potentially acquiring a specific stock at a lower price. This strategy involves selling put options with the intention of being assigned the underlying stock if the options are exercised. In this chapter, we will delve into cash-secured put writing, how it operates, its advantages, and considerations for income generation.

Definition of Cash-Secured Put Writing:

Cash-secured put writing is executed when an investor:

1. Sells (writes) put options on a specific stock.

2. Maintains sufficient cash in their brokerage account to cover the purchase of the underlying stock if the put options are exercised.

How Cash-Secured Put Writing Works:

Here is a step-by-step explanation of how cash-secured put writing operates:

1. **Selecting the Underlying Stock**: The investor identifies a stock they are interested in potentially acquiring.

2. **Put Option Sale**: The investor sells put options on the selected stock. Each put option represents the right (but not the obligation) for the option holder to sell 100 shares of the underlying stock at a specified strike price before the option's expiration date.

3. **Expiration Date and Strike Price**: The investor chooses an expiration date and strike price for the put options they sell. The strike price determines the price at which they would be obligated to buy the stock if the put options are exercised.

4. **Premium Collection**: In exchange for selling the put options, the investor receives a premium, which is credited to their brokerage account immediately. This premium serves as income.

5. **Outcomes**:

◈ If the stock price remains above the put option's strike price until expiration, the put options expire worthless, and the investor keeps the premium as income.

◈ If the stock price falls below the put option's strike price, the options may be exercised, and the investor is obligated to purchase the stock at the strike price, using the cash they have secured in their account.

Advantages of Cash-Secured Put Writing:

1. **Income Generation**: The primary goal of this strategy is to generate income through premium collection when selling put options.

2. **Potential Stock Acquisition**: Investors may acquire the underlying stock at a lower price if the put options are exercised. This can be advantageous if they are interested in owning the stock long term.

3. **Customizable Strategy**: Investors can tailor the strategy by selecting strike prices and expiration dates that align with their income goals and stock acquisition preferences.

Considerations in Cash-Secured Put Writing:

1. **Obligation to Buy**: Investors should be prepared to purchase the underlying stock at the strike price if the put options are exercised. They should only sell puts on stocks they are willing to own.

2. **Limited Profit Potential**: The profit from cash-secured put writing is limited to the premium received. Investors cap their potential gains, even if the stock rises significantly.

3. **Cash Requirements**: This strategy requires maintaining sufficient cash in the brokerage account to cover the purchase of the underlying stock if the put options are exercised.

4. **Market Conditions**: Cash-secured put writing is more effective in neutral or slightly bullish markets. In strongly bearish markets, it may result in stock acquisition, which could lead to paper losses.

5. **Risk Management**: Proper risk management is crucial. Investors should monitor their positions, set stop-loss orders, and be prepared to adjust their strategy if market conditions change.

In summary, cash-secured put writing is an income-generating strategy that combines options trading with the potential for acquiring stocks at a lower price. While it offers advantages in terms of income generation and potential stock acquisition, it comes with the obligation to buy the underlying stock if the put options are exercised. Therefore, investors should carefully consider their goals, risk tolerance, and market conditions before implementing this strategy.

Credit Spreads (Bull Put Spreads, Bear Call Spreads)

Credit spreads are versatile options strategies that traders and investors use to generate income while simultaneously managing risk. These strategies involve the simultaneous purchase and sale of options with different strike prices or expiration dates within the same option class. In this chapter, we will explore two common types of credit spreads: bull put spreads and bear call spreads, how they work, their advantages, and considerations for income generation and risk management.

Bull Put Spread (Credit Put Spread):

A bull put spread is a strategy employed when an investor expects a moderate bullish move in the underlying asset's price. This strategy involves two key steps:

1. **Short Put Option**: The investor sells (writes) a put option with a lower strike price, closer to the current market price of the underlying asset. This put option generates a premium (credit) when sold.

2. **Long Put Option**: Simultaneously, the investor purchases a put option with a higher strike price, further away from the current market price. This put option requires an upfront cost (debit).

The net result is a credit to the investor's account, hence the term "credit spread." The maximum profit occurs if the underlying asset's price remains above the higher strike price at expiration, while the maximum loss is limited to the difference in strike prices minus the initial credit received.

Bear Call Spread (Credit Call Spread):

A bear call spread is a strategy utilized when an investor anticipates a moderate bearish move in the underlying asset's price. This strategy involves two main steps:

1. **Short Call Option**: The investor sells (writes) a call option with a strike price closer to the current market price of the underlying asset. This call option generates a premium (credit) when sold.

2. **Long Call Option**: Simultaneously, the investor purchases a call option with a higher strike price, further away from the current market price. This call option requires an upfront cost (debit).

Similar to the bull put spread, the net result of the bear call spread is a credit to the investor's account. The maximum profit occurs if the underlying asset's price remains below the lower strike price at expiration, while the maximum loss is capped at the difference in strike prices minus the initial credit received.

Advantages of Credit Spreads:

1. **Income Generation**: Credit spreads generate upfront income (credit) for the investor due to the premium received when selling options.

2. **Limited Risk**: Both bull put spreads and bear call spreads have defined and limited risk. The maximum loss is known upfront and is typically lower than the potential loss from uncovered options positions.

3. **Reduced Margin Requirement**: In many cases, credit spreads require lower margin requirements than uncovered options positions, making them capital-efficient.

4. **Risk Management**: Credit spreads allow investors to take a directional view on the underlying asset while having predefined risk parameters.

Considerations in Credit Spreads:

1. **Risk-Reward Ratio**: Assess the risk-reward ratio and understand that the potential profit is limited, often less than the potential loss.

2. **Market Outlook**: Ensure that the chosen credit spread aligns with your market outlook (bullish for bull put spreads, bearish for bear call spreads).

3. **Expiration and Strike Selection**: Carefully select expiration dates and strike prices based on your outlook and risk tolerance.

4. **Management and Adjustment**: Have a plan for managing the trade, including setting stop-loss orders and considering adjustments if market conditions change.

5. **Assignment Risk**: Be aware of the possibility of early assignment, especially in American-style options. Have a plan for handling assigned positions.

In summary, credit spreads, including bull put spreads and bear call spreads, are income-generating options strategies with limited risk. They offer traders and investors a way to express a market view while collecting upfront premiums. However, it's essential to carefully consider strike prices, expiration dates, and risk management when implementing these strategies.

Iron Condors and Iron Butterflies

Iron condors and iron butterflies are advanced options strategies used by traders and investors to generate income while managing risk. These strategies involve the combination of call and put options with different strike prices and expiration dates to create a range-bound position on an underlying asset. In this chapter, we will explore both iron condors and iron butterflies, how they work, their advantages, and considerations for income generation and risk management.

Iron Condor:

An iron condor is an income-generating strategy that is suitable for markets with low volatility or when an investor expects a specific underlying asset to trade within a defined price range. This strategy involves four key options positions:

1. **Short Put**: The investor sells (writes) a put option with a strike price below the current market price of the underlying asset. This put option generates a premium (credit) when sold.

2. **Long Put**: Simultaneously, the investor purchases a put option with a lower strike price than the short put option. This put option acts as downside protection and requires an upfront cost (debit).

3. **Short Call**: The investor sells (writes) a call option with a strike price above the current market price of the underlying asset. This call option also generates a premium (credit) when sold.

4. **Long Call**: Simultaneously, the investor purchases a call option with a higher strike price than the short call option. This call option acts as upside protection and requires an upfront cost (debit).

The combination of these four positions results in a net credit to the investor's account. The maximum profit occurs if the underlying asset's price remains within the range defined by the two strike prices of the short options at expiration. The maximum loss is limited and occurs if the underlying asset's price moves significantly beyond the strike prices of the long options at expiration.

Iron Butterfly:

An iron butterfly is another range-bound income-generating strategy, but it is used when an investor expects very low volatility in the underlying asset. This strategy involves four key options positions as well:

1. **Short Put**: The investor sells (writes) a put option with a strike price at or near the current market price of the underlying asset. This put option generates a premium (credit) when sold.

2. **Long Put**: Simultaneously, the investor purchases a put option with a lower strike price than the short put option. This put option acts as downside protection and requires an upfront cost (debit).

3. **Short Call**: The investor sells (writes) a call option with a strike price at or near the current market price of the underlying asset. This call option also generates a premium (credit) when sold.

4. **Long Call**: Simultaneously, the investor purchases a call option with a higher strike price than the short call option. This call option acts as upside protection and requires an upfront cost (debit).

As with the iron condor, the combination of these four positions results in a net credit to the investor's account. The maximum profit occurs if the underlying asset's price remains near the middle strike price at expiration. The maximum loss is limited and occurs if the underlying asset's price deviates significantly from the middle strike price in either direction at expiration.

Advantages of Iron Condors and Iron Butterflies:

1. **Income Generation**: Both strategies generate income through the premiums received from selling options.

2. **Range-Bound Profits**: These strategies are designed for range-bound markets, where the underlying asset's price is expected to remain within a specified range.

3. **Limited Risk**: The maximum loss is defined and limited, making them suitable for risk management.

4. **Customizable**: Traders can tailor these strategies by selecting strike prices and expiration dates based on their market outlook.

Considerations in Iron Condors and Iron Butterflies:

1. **Market Outlook**: Ensure that the chosen strategy aligns with your market outlook, whether it's low volatility for iron butterflies or moderately low volatility for iron condors.

2. **Risk-Reward Ratio**: Assess the risk-reward ratio and understand that the potential profit is limited, often less than the potential loss.

3. **Management**: Have a plan for managing the trade, including setting stop-loss orders and considering adjustments if market conditions change.

4. **Assignment Risk**: Be aware of the possibility of early assignment, especially in American-style options.

5. **Commissions**: Consider the impact of commissions and fees on the overall profitability of these strategies.

In conclusion, iron condors and iron butterflies are income-generating options strategies designed for range-bound markets with varying levels of volatility. They offer advantages in terms of defined risk and customizable positions but require careful consideration of market conditions, strike prices, and risk management techniques. Traders and investors should have a clear understanding of their market expectations and risk tolerance when implementing these strategies.

Dividend Capture Strategies

Dividend capture strategies are a specialized approach employed by traders and investors to capture dividends paid by stocks while optimizing the use of capital and managing risk. These strategies are particularly popular among income-focused market participants seeking to profit from dividend payments without necessarily holding the stock for an extended period. In this chapter, we will explore dividend capture strategies, how they work, their advantages, and considerations for income generation and risk management.

Definition of Dividend Capture Strategies:

Dividend capture strategies involve a series of actions taken to buy and sell a stock with the primary goal of capturing the dividend payment. These strategies aim to benefit from the dividend without necessarily having a long-term investment thesis for the stock.

How Dividend Capture Strategies Work:

Dividend capture strategies typically follow this sequence of actions:

1. **Timing**: The investor identifies stocks with upcoming dividend payments and selects those that fit their strategy.

2. **Purchase**: Before the ex-dividend date (the date on which a stock's shares begin trading without the dividend), the investor buys the stock.

3. **Ex-Dividend Date**: On the ex-dividend date, the stock begins trading without the dividend. The investor must hold the stock at this time to be eligible to receive the dividend.

4. **Sell**: After capturing the dividend, which is typically a fixed amount per share, the investor sells the stock.

5. **Profit**: The profit is generated from the dividend payment, and the investor can then decide whether to repeat the process with other dividend-paying stocks.

Advantages of Dividend Capture Strategies:

1. **Income Generation**: The primary advantage is income generation through the receipt of dividends.

2. **Shorter Holding Period**: Investors do not need to hold the stock for an extended period, making capital available for other opportunities.

3. **Predictable Income**: Dividend amounts and ex-dividend dates are typically known in advance, providing predictability.

4. **Diversification**: Investors can diversify across different dividend-paying stocks to manage risk.

Considerations in Dividend Capture Strategies:

1. **Ex-Dividend Date**: Timing is crucial in dividend capture strategies. Ensure that the stock is purchased before the ex-dividend date to be eligible for the dividend.

2. **Transaction Costs**: Consider transaction costs such as commissions and fees, which can impact the overall profitability of the strategy.

3. **Market Risk**: Be aware of market risk, as stock prices can fluctuate significantly, potentially affecting the strategy's profitability.

4. **Tax Implications**: Dividend income may have tax consequences. Consult a tax advisor to understand the tax implications of dividend capture strategies.

5. **Diversification**: Diversify the portfolio to spread risk across different stocks and sectors.

6. **Stock Selection**: Carefully select dividend-paying stocks based on your income goals and risk tolerance.

7. **Opportunity Cost**: Capital tied up in dividend capture strategies may not be available for other investment opportunities.

8. **Dividend Cuts**: Be aware that companies may cut or suspend dividends, which can impact the strategy's profitability.

In summary, dividend capture strategies are designed to generate income by capturing dividends paid by stocks. These strategies are attractive to income-focused investors seeking to optimize their use of capital and manage risk. However, they require careful timing, consideration of transaction costs, and an understanding of market and tax implications. Traders and investors should align their strategy with their income goals and risk tolerance when implementing dividend capture strategies.

Chapter 6: Directional Option Strategies

Long Calls and Puts

Long calls and long puts are fundamental directional option strategies that traders and investors employ when they anticipate significant price movements in the underlying asset. These strategies offer the potential for substantial profits but come with limited risk, as the maximum loss is limited to the premium paid for the options. In this chapter, we will explore both long calls and long puts, how they work, their advantages, and considerations for implementing these strategies.

Long Call Strategy:

A long call strategy is employed when an investor expects the price of the underlying asset to rise significantly. This strategy involves purchasing call options, which grant the buyer the right (but not the obligation) to buy the underlying asset at a specified strike price before the option's expiration date. Key points about the long call strategy include:

1. **Buy Call Options**: The investor buys call options with a specific strike price and expiration date, paying a premium for each option.

2. **Profit Potential**: The profit potential is theoretically unlimited, as the call option allows the investor to participate in the underlying asset's price increase.

3. **Limited Risk**: The maximum loss is limited to the premium paid for the call options. This limited risk makes long calls an attractive strategy for traders seeking leveraged exposure to a price increase.

4. **Breakeven**: The breakeven point is the strike price plus the premium paid for the call option. The underlying asset's price must rise above this level for the strategy to be profitable.

Advantages of Long Call Strategy:

1. **Profit Potential**: Long calls offer the potential for significant profits if the underlying asset's price rises substantially.

2. **Limited Risk**: The maximum loss is capped at the premium paid, providing risk control.

3. **Leverage**: Long calls provide leveraged exposure to price movements, allowing investors to control a larger position with a relatively small upfront investment.

Considerations in Long Call Strategy:

1. **Time Decay**: The value of call options erodes over time due to time decay. Therefore, it's crucial to be mindful of the time remaining until expiration.

2. **Market Direction**: Long calls are profitable when the underlying asset's price rises. If the price remains flat or declines, the premium paid for the options may be lost.

3. **Volatility**: Higher volatility can increase the premium cost of options, potentially impacting the profitability of the strategy.

4. **Exit Strategy**: Have a clear exit strategy, including profit-taking and stop-loss levels, to manage the trade effectively.

Long Put Strategy:

A long put strategy is employed when an investor expects the price of the underlying asset to decline significantly. This strategy involves purchasing put options, which grant the buyer the right (but not the obligation) to sell the underlying asset at a specified strike price before the option's expiration date. Key points about the long put strategy include:

1. **Buy Put Options**: The investor buys put options with a specific strike price and expiration date, paying a premium for each option.

2. **Profit Potential**: The profit potential is theoretically unlimited, as the put option allows the investor to profit from the underlying asset's price decline.

3. **Limited Risk**: The maximum loss is limited to the premium paid for the put options. This limited risk makes long puts an attractive strategy for traders seeking to profit from price declines.

4. **Breakeven**: The breakeven point is the strike price minus the premium paid for the put option. The underlying asset's price must fall below this level for the strategy to be profitable.

Advantages of Long Put Strategy:

1. **Profit Potential**: Long puts offer the potential for significant profits if the underlying asset's price falls substantially.

2. **Limited Risk**: The maximum loss is capped at the premium paid, providing risk control.

3. **Hedging**: Long puts can be used to hedge an existing long position in the underlying asset, providing downside protection.

Considerations in Long Put Strategy:

1. **Time Decay**: Similar to long calls, the value of put options erodes over time due to time decay. Be mindful of the time remaining until expiration.

2. **Market Direction**: Long puts are profitable when the underlying asset's price falls. If the price remains flat or rises, the premium paid for the options may be lost.

3. **Volatility**: Higher volatility can increase the premium cost of options, potentially impacting the profitability of the strategy.

4. **Exit Strategy**: Develop a clear exit strategy, including profit-taking and stop-loss levels, to manage the trade effectively.

In summary, long calls and long puts are directional option strategies used to profit from anticipated price movements in the underlying asset. Long calls benefit from price increases, while long puts benefit from price declines. These strategies offer substantial profit potential with limited risk, making them popular choices among traders and investors with directional views on the market. However, it's essential to consider factors such as time decay, market direction, and volatility when implementing these strategies and to have a well-defined exit plan.

Call and Put Diagonals

Call and put diagonal spreads, also known as diagonal calendar spreads, are versatile directional option strategies that combine elements of time decay and volatility to profit from specific price movements in the underlying asset. These strategies involve the simultaneous purchase and sale of options with different strike prices and expiration dates. In this chapter, we will explore both call and put diagonal spreads, how they work, their advantages, and considerations for implementing these strategies.

Call Diagonal Spread:

A call diagonal spread is a strategy employed when an investor expects the price of the underlying asset to have a moderate upward movement. This strategy involves two key steps:

1. **Long Call Option**: The investor buys a call option with a longer-term expiration date and a strike price that reflects their outlook for the underlying asset's future price.

2. **Short Call Option**: Simultaneously, the investor sells a call option with a closer-to-the-money strike price and a shorter-term expiration date. This short call option generates a premium (credit) when sold.

The net result is a debit to the investor's account, as the long call option typically costs more than the premium received from selling the short call option. The maximum profit occurs if the underlying asset's price rises to the strike price of the short call option at expiration. The maximum loss is limited to the net debit paid for the spread.

Put Diagonal Spread:

A put diagonal spread is used when an investor expects the price of the underlying asset to experience a moderate downward movement. This strategy involves two key steps:

1. **Long Put Option**: The investor buys a put option with a longer-term expiration date and a strike price that aligns with their bearish outlook for the underlying asset's future price.

2. **Short Put Option**: Simultaneously, the investor sells a put option with a closer-to-the-money strike price and a shorter-term expiration date. This short put option generates a premium (credit) when sold.

Similar to the call diagonal spread, the net result of the put diagonal spread is a debit to the investor's account. The maximum profit occurs if the underlying asset's price declines to the strike price of the short put option at expiration. The maximum loss is limited to the net debit paid for the spread.

Advantages of Diagonal Spreads:

1. **Income Generation**: Diagonal spreads generate income through the premiums received from selling options.

2. **Time Decay**: The strategy benefits from time decay, as the short-term option loses value more quickly than the longer-term option.

3. **Limited Risk**: The maximum loss is capped at the net debit paid for the spread, providing risk control.

4. **Customizable**: Investors can tailor these strategies by selecting strike prices and expiration dates based on their market outlook.

Considerations in Diagonal Spreads:

1. **Market Outlook**: Ensure that the chosen diagonal spread aligns with your market outlook (bullish for call diagonals, bearish for put diagonals).

2. **Time Decay**: Be aware that time decay works against the short-term option, so monitor the position and consider adjustments as expiration approaches.

3. **Volatility**: Changes in volatility can impact the profitability of diagonal spreads, particularly the short-term option.

4. **Transaction Costs**: Consider the impact of commissions and fees on the overall profitability of these strategies.

5. **Management**: Have a clear exit and adjustment strategy, including profit-taking and stop-loss levels, to manage the trade effectively.

In summary, call and put diagonal spreads are directional option strategies that benefit from specific price movements in the underlying asset while capitalizing on time decay. These strategies offer income generation and risk control with limited potential loss. However, they require careful consideration of market conditions, time decay, and volatility. Traders and investors should align their strategy with their directional outlook and risk tolerance when implementing diagonal spreads.

Synthetic Positions

Synthetic positions are advanced options strategies that replicate the risk and reward characteristics of owning or shorting an underlying asset while using a combination of options. These strategies are versatile and can be used for various purposes, including speculation, hedging, and capital efficiency. In this chapter, we will explore synthetic long and short positions, how they work, their advantages, and considerations for implementing these strategies.

Synthetic Long Position:

A synthetic long position is created to mimic the risk and reward profile of owning the underlying asset. It is typically employed when an investor expects the price of the underlying asset to rise. A synthetic long position can be constructed using the following components:

1. **Long Call Option**: The investor buys a call option on the underlying asset. This call option gives the investor the right to buy the asset at a specified strike price.

2. **Short Put Option**: Simultaneously, the investor sells a put option on the same underlying asset with the same strike price as the call option. This put option obligates the investor to buy the asset at the strike price if the option is exercised.

The combination of the long call and short put creates a position that behaves like owning the underlying asset. The maximum loss is limited to the difference between the strike price and the premium received from selling the put option. The maximum profit is theoretically unlimited as the asset's price rises.

Synthetic Short Position:

A synthetic short position is designed to replicate the risk and reward profile of shorting the underlying asset. It is typically used when an investor expects the price of the underlying asset to decline. A synthetic short position can be created using the following components:

1. **Short Call Option**: The investor sells (writes) a call option on the underlying asset. This call option obligates the investor to sell the asset at a specified strike price if the option is exercised.

2. **Long Put Option**: Simultaneously, the investor buys a put option on the same underlying asset with the same strike price as the call option. This put option gives the investor the right to sell the asset at the strike price.

The combination of the short call and long put creates a position that behaves like shorting the underlying asset. The maximum loss is limited to the difference between the strike price and the premium paid for the put option. The maximum profit is theoretically unlimited as the asset's price declines.

Advantages of Synthetic Positions:

1. **Risk Management**: Synthetic positions provide a way to manage risk while achieving similar market exposure as owning or shorting the underlying asset.

2. **Capital Efficiency**: These strategies often require less capital compared to directly owning or shorting the asset.

3. **Versatility**: Synthetic positions can be customized for various market outlooks, including bullish, bearish, or neutral views.

4. **Leverage**: Depending on the strike prices and premiums involved, synthetic positions can offer leverage, amplifying potential returns.

Considerations in Synthetic Positions:

1. **Option Selection**: Carefully choose the strike prices and expiration dates for the call and put options to align with your market outlook and risk tolerance.

2. **Time Decay**: Be aware that options have time decay, which can impact the profitability of synthetic positions.

3. **Volatility**: Changes in volatility can affect the profitability of these strategies, particularly the short options.

4. **Assignment Risk**: Understand the possibility of early assignment, especially with American-style options.

5. **Management**: Develop a clear exit and adjustment strategy, including profit-taking and stop-loss levels, to manage the synthetic position effectively.

In summary, synthetic positions are versatile options strategies that replicate the risk and reward characteristics of owning or shorting the underlying asset. These strategies offer risk management, capital efficiency, and flexibility for traders and investors with specific market outlooks. However, they require careful consideration of option selection, time decay, volatility, and assignment risk. Traders and investors should align their strategy with their market expectations and risk tolerance when implementing synthetic positions.

Ratio Spreads (Call Ratio Spread, Put Ratio Spread)

Ratio spreads are advanced directional option strategies that involve a combination of buying and selling call or put options on the same underlying asset. These strategies are employed when an investor expects a specific price movement in the underlying asset but wants to customize the risk and reward profile of the trade. In this chapter, we will explore both call ratio spreads and put ratio spreads, how they work, their advantages, and considerations for implementing these strategies.

Call Ratio Spread:

A call ratio spread is a strategy employed when an investor anticipates a moderate upward price movement in the underlying asset. This strategy involves the following components:

1. **Long Calls**: The investor buys a certain number of call options on the underlying asset. These calls typically have the same strike price and expiration date.

2. **Short Calls**: Simultaneously, the investor sells a greater number of call options on the same underlying asset with the same strike price but a higher expiration date. The number of short calls sold exceeds the number of long calls bought.

The net result is a net credit to the investor's account, as the premium received from selling the additional short calls should be higher than the premium paid for the long calls. The strategy's risk and reward characteristics are customized based on the number of short calls relative to long calls.

Put Ratio Spread:

A put ratio spread is employed when an investor expects a moderate downward price movement in the underlying asset. This strategy involves the following components:

1. **Long Puts**: The investor buys a certain number of put options on the underlying asset. These puts typically have the same strike price and expiration date.

2. **Short Puts**: Simultaneously, the investor sells a greater number of put options on the same underlying asset with the same strike price but a lower expiration date. The number of short puts sold exceeds the number of long puts bought.

Similar to the call ratio spread, the net result of the put ratio spread is a net credit to the investor's account. The strategy's risk and reward characteristics are adjusted based on the number of short puts relative to long puts.

Advantages of Ratio Spreads:

1. **Customization**: Ratio spreads allow investors to tailor the risk and reward profile of their trade to align with their market outlook.

2. **Income Generation**: These strategies often result in a net credit, providing income to the investor.

3. **Reduced Cost**: By selling more options than they buy, investors can reduce the upfront cost or even create a credit position.

4. **Profit Potential**: Ratio spreads offer the potential for profits both in the direction of the anticipated price movement and through time decay.

Considerations in Ratio Spreads:

1. **Strike Selection**: Carefully choose the strike prices for the long and short options to match the desired risk and reward profile.

2. **Assignment Risk**: Understand the possibility of early assignment, especially with American-style options.

3. **Adjustments**: Develop a clear plan for managing the trade, including adjustments if market conditions change.

4. **Market Outlook**: Ensure that the chosen ratio spread aligns with your market outlook (bullish for call ratio spreads, bearish for put ratio spreads).

5. **Time Decay**: Monitor the position's exposure to time decay, as it can impact profitability.

6. **Volatility**: Changes in volatility can affect the profitability of these strategies, particularly the short options.

In summary, ratio spreads, including call ratio spreads and put ratio spreads, are advanced directional option strategies that provide customization of risk and reward profiles. These strategies are suitable for investors with specific market expectations and offer income generation potential. However, they require careful consideration of strike selection, assignment risk, adjustments, and market conditions. Traders and investors should align their strategy with their market outlook and risk tolerance when implementing ratio spreads.

Long Straddle and Strangle

Long straddle and long strangle are versatile options strategies employed by traders and investors when they anticipate significant price volatility in the underlying asset. These strategies involve buying both call and put options simultaneously to profit from substantial price movements, regardless of the direction. In this chapter, we will explore both long straddle and long strangle strategies, how they work, their advantages, and considerations for implementing these strategies.

Long Straddle:

A long straddle is a strategy employed when an investor expects significant price volatility in the underlying asset but is uncertain about the direction of the price movement. This strategy involves two key steps:

1. **Long Call Option**: The investor buys a call option on the underlying asset with a specific strike price and expiration date.

2. **Long Put Option**: Simultaneously, the investor buys a put option on the same underlying asset with the same strike price and expiration date as the call option.

The net result is a debit to the investor's account, as both the call and put options have premiums that must be paid. The maximum loss is limited to the total premium paid for the straddle. The maximum profit potential is theoretically unlimited in both directions, as the strategy profits from significant price movement, whether up or down.

Long Strangle:

A long strangle is similar to a long straddle but is used when the investor expects significant price volatility in the underlying asset and is willing to accept a lower upfront cost. This strategy involves two key steps:

1. **Long Call Option**: The investor buys a call option on the underlying asset with a higher strike price than the current market price and a specific expiration date.

2. **Long Put Option**: Simultaneously, the investor buys a put option on the same underlying asset with a lower strike price than the current market price and the same expiration date as the call option.

Like the long straddle, the net result of the long strangle is a debit to the investor's account, but the cost is typically lower due to the difference in strike prices. The maximum loss is limited to the total premium paid for the strangle. The maximum profit potential is theoretically unlimited in both directions, as the strategy profits from significant price movement.

Advantages of Long Straddle and Strangle:

1. **Profit from Volatility**: These strategies excel in highly volatile markets, as they profit from significant price movement, regardless of direction.

2. **Hedging**: Long straddles and strangles can be used as portfolio protection against unexpected market events.

3. **Leverage**: These strategies offer leveraged exposure to price movements with a limited upfront cost.

4. **Customizable**: Investors can tailor the strategy by selecting strike prices and expiration dates based on their market outlook.

Considerations in Long Straddle and Strangle:

1. **Volatility**: These strategies require substantial price movement to be profitable, so be aware of the level of volatility in the underlying asset.

2. **Time Decay**: Time decay can erode the value of the options, particularly if the anticipated price movement does not occur quickly.

3. **Cost**: Consider the total premium paid for the straddle or strangle, as it represents the maximum potential loss.

4. **Exit Strategy**: Develop a clear exit plan, including profit-taking and stop-loss levels, to manage the trade effectively.

5. **Market Outlook**: Ensure that the chosen strategy aligns with your market outlook (expecting high volatility).

In summary, long straddle and long strangle are directional options strategies used to profit from significant price volatility in the underlying asset. These strategies offer the potential for unlimited profits in both directions but come with the risk of time decay and cost. Traders and investors should carefully consider the level of volatility, time decay, and cost when implementing straddle and strangle strategies and have a well-defined exit plan.

Chapter 7: Volatility Trading Strategies

Volatility Arbitrage

Volatility arbitrage is an advanced trading strategy employed by traders and investors to profit from discrepancies in implied volatility levels among related financial instruments. This strategy relies on the premise that implied volatility, which represents market expectations of future price fluctuations, can deviate from historical or realized volatility. Volatility arbitrage aims to capture these discrepancies by simultaneously trading options or other derivatives to exploit differences in implied volatility. In this chapter, we will explore volatility arbitrage, how it works, its advantages, and considerations for implementing this strategy.

Definition of Volatility Arbitrage:

Volatility arbitrage involves trading options, volatility derivatives, or related instruments to capitalize on differences between implied volatility and historical volatility or differences in implied volatility among related assets or instruments.

How Volatility Arbitrage Works:

Volatility arbitrage strategies can vary, but they generally involve the following steps:

1. **Identify Discrepancies**: The trader or investor identifies instances where implied volatility differs from historical or realized volatility or where implied volatility varies among related assets.

2. **Construct Positions**: Based on the identified discrepancies, the trader constructs positions that involve buying or selling options, volatility derivatives, or other instruments.

3. **Profit from Convergence**: The goal is to profit as the implied volatility converges or adjusts to more accurately reflect the underlying market conditions. The trader may then unwind their positions to realize a profit.

Advantages of Volatility Arbitrage:

1. **Profit Potential**: Volatility arbitrage offers profit potential from the convergence of implied volatility, regardless of the direction of the underlying asset's price.

2. **Diversification**: This strategy can be applied to a wide range of assets, providing diversification opportunities.

3. **Risk Management**: By trading options and related instruments, traders can manage and limit their risk exposure.

4. **Market Neutral**: Some volatility arbitrage strategies can be market-neutral, meaning they are not dependent on the overall market direction.

Considerations in Volatility Arbitrage:

1. **Data Analysis**: Accurate data analysis and modeling of implied and historical volatility are crucial for identifying arbitrage opportunities.

2. **Liquidity**: Ensure that the options or derivatives being traded have sufficient liquidity to execute the strategy effectively.

3. **Timing**: Timing is critical in volatility arbitrage, as implied volatility can change rapidly.

4. **Costs**: Be mindful of transaction costs, commissions, and fees, which can impact the overall profitability of the strategy.

5. **Risk Management**: Implement risk management techniques, including stop-loss orders, to limit potential losses.

6. **Market Events**: Be aware of market events, earnings announcements, or economic releases that can impact implied volatility.

7. **Regulatory Considerations**: Familiarize yourself with regulatory requirements related to options and derivatives trading in your jurisdiction.

In summary, volatility arbitrage is an advanced trading strategy designed to capitalize on discrepancies in implied volatility levels among related financial instruments. This strategy offers profit potential from the convergence of implied volatility and can be applied to a variety of assets. However, it requires accurate data analysis, attention to timing, risk management, and an understanding of transaction costs and market events. Traders and investors should carefully assess arbitrage opportunities and implement appropriate risk controls when engaging in volatility arbitrage.

Volatility ETPs (Exchange-Traded Products)

Volatility Exchange-Traded Products (ETPs), also known as Volatility ETFs (Exchange-Traded Funds) or ETNs (Exchange-Traded Notes), are specialized financial instruments designed to provide exposure to market volatility as an asset class. These products track volatility indexes, such as the VIX (CBOE Volatility Index), and can be used by traders and investors to speculate on or hedge against changes in market volatility. In this chapter, we will explore Volatility ETPs, how they work, their advantages, and considerations for implementing these instruments.

Definition of Volatility ETPs:

Volatility ETPs are investment products that aim to replicate the performance of volatility indexes, which measure the expected volatility of the stock market. These ETPs are designed to provide traders and investors with direct exposure to market volatility.

How Volatility ETPs Work:

Volatility ETPs are structured to achieve their investment objectives through futures contracts or options on volatility indexes. Here's a general overview of how they work:

1. **Underlying Index**: Volatility ETPs track specific volatility indexes, with the VIX being one of the most widely followed. These indexes measure expected market volatility based on the implied volatility of options on a particular benchmark index, such as the S&P 500.

2. **Futures Contracts**: Some Volatility ETPs use futures contracts on the underlying volatility index to gain exposure. They can either hold these futures contracts directly or roll them over to maintain exposure.

3. **Options Contracts**: Other Volatility ETPs use options on the volatility index to achieve their objectives. These options may be used for hedging or speculative purposes.

4. **Leverage and Inverse**: Some Volatility ETPs provide leveraged or inverse exposure to the underlying index, allowing traders to amplify returns or bet on a decrease in volatility.

5. **Daily Resets**: Leveraged and inverse Volatility ETPs typically reset daily, which can lead to tracking errors over longer periods due to compounding effects.

Advantages of Volatility ETPs:

1. **Diversification**: Volatility ETPs offer diversification benefits as they are linked to the volatility of the broader market, not individual stocks.

2. **Hedging**: Investors can use Volatility ETPs to hedge against market volatility, helping protect their portfolios during turbulent times.

3. **Speculation**: Traders can use these instruments to speculate on short-term volatility fluctuations, potentially profiting from market turmoil.

4. **Liquidity**: Many Volatility ETPs are highly liquid and can be easily traded on stock exchanges, providing flexibility for investors.

5. **Transparency**: ETPs provide transparency in terms of holdings, net asset value (NAV), and trading prices.

Considerations in Volatility ETPs:

1. **Short-Term Nature**: Volatility ETPs are primarily designed for short-term trading or hedging, and they may not perform as expected over longer periods due to compounding effects.

2. **Understanding the Underlying Index**: Traders and investors should have a thorough understanding of the underlying volatility index and its characteristics.

3. **Risk Management**: The use of leveraged or inverse Volatility ETPs can magnify gains and losses, so risk management is essential.

4. **Tracking Errors**: Due to daily resets and costs associated with futures or options, the performance of leveraged or inverse Volatility ETPs can deviate from the underlying index.

5. **Volatility Timing**: Successfully trading Volatility ETPs requires accurate timing and analysis of market volatility trends.

6. **Tax Considerations**: Tax implications can vary depending on the structure and holding period of Volatility ETPs, so consult a tax advisor.

In summary, Volatility ETPs are specialized financial instruments that provide exposure to market volatility as an asset class. They can be used for diversification, hedging, speculation, or risk management. However, due to their short-term nature and potential for tracking errors, traders and investors should approach these products with a clear understanding of their goals and risk tolerance. Additionally, leverage and inverse ETPs should be used cautiously and with proper risk management strategies.

Volatility ETPs (Exchange-Traded Products)

Volatility Exchange-Traded Products (ETPs), also known as Volatility ETFs (Exchange-Traded Funds) or ETNs (Exchange-Traded Notes), are specialized financial instruments designed to provide exposure to market volatility as an asset class. These products track volatility indexes, such as the VIX (CBOE Volatility Index), and can be used by traders and investors to speculate on or hedge against changes in market volatility. In this chapter, we will explore Volatility ETPs, how they work, their advantages, and considerations for implementing these instruments.

Definition of Volatility ETPs:

Volatility ETPs are investment products that aim to replicate the performance of volatility indexes, which measure the expected volatility of the stock market. These ETPs are designed to provide traders and investors with direct exposure to market volatility.

How Volatility ETPs Work:

Volatility ETPs are structured to achieve their investment objectives through futures contracts or options on volatility indexes. Here's a general overview of how they work:

1. **Underlying Index**: Volatility ETPs track specific volatility indexes, with the VIX being one of the most widely followed. These indexes measure expected market volatility based on the implied volatility of options on a particular benchmark index, such as the S&P 500.

2. **Futures Contracts**: Some Volatility ETPs use futures contracts on the underlying volatility index to gain exposure. They can either hold these futures contracts directly or roll them over to maintain exposure.

3. **Options Contracts**: Other Volatility ETPs use options on the volatility index to achieve their objectives. These options may be used for hedging or speculative purposes.

4. **Leverage and Inverse**: Some Volatility ETPs provide leveraged or inverse exposure to the underlying index, allowing traders to amplify returns or bet on a decrease in volatility.

5. **Daily Resets**: Leveraged and inverse Volatility ETPs typically reset daily, which can lead to tracking errors over longer periods due to compounding effects.

Advantages of Volatility ETPs:

1. **Diversification**: Volatility ETPs offer diversification benefits as they are linked to the volatility of the broader market, not individual stocks.

2. **Hedging**: Investors can use Volatility ETPs to hedge against market volatility, helping protect their portfolios during turbulent times.

3. **Speculation**: Traders can use these instruments to speculate on short-term volatility fluctuations, potentially profiting from market turmoil.

4. **Liquidity**: Many Volatility ETPs are highly liquid and can be easily traded on stock exchanges, providing flexibility for investors.

5. **Transparency**: ETPs provide transparency in terms of holdings, net asset value (NAV), and trading prices.

Considerations in Volatility ETPs:

1. **Short-Term Nature**: Volatility ETPs are primarily designed for short-term trading or hedging, and they may not perform as expected over longer periods due to compounding effects.

2. **Understanding the Underlying Index**: Traders and investors should have a thorough understanding of the underlying volatility index and its characteristics.

3. **Risk Management**: The use of leveraged or inverse Volatility ETPs can magnify gains and losses, so risk management is essential.

4. **Tracking Errors**: Due to daily resets and costs associated with futures or options, the performance of leveraged or inverse Volatility ETPs can deviate from the underlying index.

5. **Volatility Timing**: Successfully trading Volatility ETPs requires accurate timing and analysis of market volatility trends.

6. **Tax Considerations**: Tax implications can vary depending on the structure and holding period of Volatility ETPs, so consult a tax advisor.

In summary, Volatility ETPs are specialized financial instruments that provide exposure to market volatility as an asset class. They can be used for diversification, hedging, speculation, or risk management. However, due to their short-term nature and potential for tracking errors, traders and investors should approach these products with a clear understanding of their goals and risk tolerance. Additionally, leverage and inverse ETPs should be used cautiously and with proper risk management strategies.

VIX Options and VIX Futures

VIX options and VIX futures are specialized financial instruments designed to provide exposure to market volatility, specifically the CBOE Volatility Index (VIX), often referred to as the "fear gauge." These instruments allow traders and investors to directly trade or hedge against changes in expected market volatility. In this chapter, we will explore VIX options and VIX futures, how they work, their advantages, and considerations for implementing these instruments.

VIX Options:

VIX options are options contracts whose underlying asset is the VIX, which represents expected market volatility. These options allow traders to speculate on or hedge against changes in market volatility. Here's how VIX options work:

1. **Underlying Index**: The underlying asset of VIX options is the VIX itself, which reflects market expectations of future volatility.

2. **Call and Put Options**: Like traditional options, VIX options come in both call and put varieties.

3. **Volatility as an Underlying**: The value of VIX options is determined by the level of volatility in the market. When market volatility increases, the value of VIX call options tends to rise, while the value of VIX put options tends to decline.

4. **Expiration**: VIX options have specific expiration dates, similar to other options contracts.

VIX Futures:

VIX futures are futures contracts whose value is tied to the VIX index. They allow traders to speculate on future levels of market volatility and can be used for hedging purposes. Here's how VIX futures work:

1. **Underlying Index**: The underlying asset of VIX futures is the VIX index.

2. **Contract Expiration**: VIX futures contracts have predefined expiration dates.

3. **Settlement**: VIX futures contracts are cash-settled. Settlement is determined based on the level of the VIX index at expiration.

4. **Volatility Expectations**: The price of VIX futures reflects the market's expectations of future volatility. If traders anticipate higher volatility in the future, VIX futures prices will be higher.

Advantages of VIX Options and VIX Futures:

1. **Direct Volatility Exposure**: These instruments offer direct exposure to market volatility as an asset class.

2. **Hedging**: Traders and investors can use VIX options and VIX futures to hedge against market volatility and protect their portfolios.

3. **Speculation**: These instruments allow for speculation on future market volatility trends, potentially profiting from market turmoil.

4. **Liquidity**: VIX options and VIX futures are generally liquid and can be traded on futures and options exchanges.

5. **Portfolio Diversification**: They provide a way to diversify a portfolio by adding exposure to volatility, which may not be correlated with traditional asset classes.

Considerations in VIX Options and VIX Futures:

1. **Volatility Timing**: Successfully trading VIX options and VIX futures requires accurate timing and analysis of market volatility trends.

2. **Risk Management**: Due to the leveraged nature of futures contracts, risk management is essential when trading VIX futures.

3. **Market Events**: Be aware of market events, earnings announcements, or economic releases that can impact implied volatility and VIX levels.

4. **Leverage**: VIX futures often involve leverage, which can amplify both gains and losses, so use proper risk management techniques.

5. **Expiration and Rollover**: Traders must be mindful of expiration dates for VIX options and futures and manage rollovers if holding positions over time.

6. **Understanding the VIX Index**: A deep understanding of how the VIX index is calculated and its characteristics is essential for effective trading.

In summary, VIX options and VIX futures provide traders and investors with a direct way to gain exposure to market volatility. They can be used for speculative purposes, hedging against volatility, and portfolio diversification. However, trading these instruments requires a solid understanding of volatility dynamics, proper risk management, and accurate timing. Traders should carefully consider their objectives and risk tolerance when trading VIX options and VIX futures.

Volatility Trading Pitfalls

Trading volatility can be rewarding, but it also presents unique challenges and risks. Understanding and navigating these pitfalls is crucial for successful volatility trading. In this chapter, we will explore common pitfalls associated with volatility trading and provide insights on how to avoid or mitigate them.

1. Underestimating the Complexity:

Pitfall: Volatility trading is complex and often requires a deep understanding of options, derivatives, and market dynamics. Traders may underestimate the complexity involved.

Mitigation: Invest time in learning about options and volatility-related instruments. Consider starting with simpler strategies before venturing into more advanced techniques. Education and practice are key.

2. Ignoring Risk Management:

Pitfall: Volatility trading can be highly leveraged, which means both gains and losses can be magnified. Traders may neglect risk management, leading to significant losses.

Mitigation: Implement robust risk management strategies, including setting stop-loss orders, defining position sizes, and diversifying your trading portfolio. Avoid over-leveraging, as it can wipe out capital quickly.

3. Neglecting Volatility Regimes:

Pitfall: Volatility is not constant; it moves in cycles. Traders may not adapt their strategies to changing volatility regimes and continue with a one-size-fits-all approach.

Mitigation: Be aware of the current volatility regime and adjust your trading strategy accordingly. Strategies that work well in high volatility environments may not be suitable for low volatility periods.

4. Overtrading:

Pitfall: Overtrading is a common pitfall in all forms of trading, including volatility trading. Traders may feel compelled to enter multiple positions, leading to higher transaction costs and emotional exhaustion.

Mitigation: Develop a disciplined trading plan with specific entry and exit criteria. Stick to your plan and avoid impulsive trades. Consider using trading journals to track your decisions and their outcomes.

5. Misinterpreting the VIX:

Pitfall: The VIX, while widely followed, is not a perfect predictor of market movements. Traders may misinterpret its signals or rely solely on it for trading decisions.

Mitigation: Use the VIX as one tool among many in your trading toolbox. Combine it with other technical and fundamental analysis to make informed decisions.

6. Failing to Account for Transaction Costs:

Pitfall: Trading options and other volatility-related instruments often involves multiple transactions, leading to higher transaction costs. Traders may not account for these costs when assessing profitability.

Mitigation: Factor in transaction costs when evaluating the profitability of your trades. Consider using cost-efficient trading platforms and strategies that minimize turnover.

7. Lack of a Clear Trading Plan:

Pitfall: Trading without a clear plan is a recipe for disaster. Traders may enter positions without predefined entry and exit points, leading to impulsive and emotional decisions.

Mitigation: Develop a well-defined trading plan that outlines your objectives, risk tolerance, entry and exit criteria, and position sizing. Stick to your plan and avoid deviating from it based on emotions.

8. Over-optimization:

Pitfall: Traders may engage in excessive optimization of their strategies, trying to fit them perfectly to historical data. This can lead to strategies that perform well in the past but poorly in the future.

Mitigation: Avoid over-optimization by focusing on robust strategies with a solid theoretical foundation. Be cautious about curve-fitting to historical data, and prioritize adaptability to changing market conditions.

9. Neglecting Fundamental Analysis:

Pitfall: Traders may become overly focused on technical indicators and volatility data while neglecting broader fundamental analysis, such as economic factors or geopolitical events.

Mitigation: Incorporate fundamental analysis into your trading approach. Consider how macroeconomic events and news can impact market sentiment and volatility.

10. Lack of Emotional Discipline:

Pitfall: Volatility trading can be emotionally challenging due to rapid price movements. Traders may make impulsive decisions driven by fear or greed.

Mitigation: Develop emotional discipline by following your trading plan, maintaining a calm mindset, and avoiding impulsive actions. Consider using mindfulness techniques to manage stress.

In conclusion, volatility trading offers opportunities for profit, but it also presents unique challenges. Traders can mitigate these pitfalls by educating themselves, practicing disciplined risk management, adapting to changing market conditions, and maintaining emotional discipline. Success in volatility trading requires a well-thought-out approach and a commitment to continuous improvement.

Chapter 8: Risk Management in Options Trading

Options Position Sizing and Portfolio Diversification

Risk management is a critical component of successful options trading. Properly sizing your positions and diversifying your options portfolio can help mitigate risk and enhance your long-term trading success. In this chapter, we will explore options position sizing and portfolio diversification strategies.

Options Position Sizing:

Options position sizing refers to determining the appropriate number of contracts or options to trade in a specific strategy. Proper position sizing is crucial to limit potential losses and manage risk effectively. Here are key considerations for options position sizing:

1. **Risk Tolerance**: Assess your risk tolerance and establish a maximum allowable loss per trade. This will help determine the size of your positions.

2. **Account Size**: Consider the size of your trading account. Avoid risking a significant percentage of your account on a single trade.

3. **Strategy Specifics**: Different options strategies have varying risk profiles. For example, a simple long call or put has limited risk, while selling naked options carries significant risk. Adjust your position size accordingly.

4. **Volatility**: Highly volatile markets may require smaller position sizes to accommodate larger price swings.

5. **Stop-Loss Orders**: Implement stop-loss orders to limit potential losses on each trade. Adjust your position size based on the stop-loss level.

6. **Liquidity**: Ensure that the options you're trading have sufficient liquidity. Illiquid options can result in unfavorable fills and slippage.

7. **Diversification**: Avoid over-concentration in a single stock or asset. Diversify your options positions across different underlying assets or sectors.

8. **Options Premium**: Consider the cost of options premiums. Smaller accounts may need to focus on lower-cost strategies or use spreads to manage premium expenses.

Portfolio Diversification:

Portfolio diversification involves spreading your options positions across different underlying assets, sectors, or strategies to reduce risk. Diversification can help protect your capital from the impact of adverse price movements in a single asset. Here are key aspects of portfolio diversification:

1. **Asset Classes**: Diversify your options portfolio across different asset classes, such as equities, commodities, and currencies. Each asset class may have its own risk and return characteristics.

2. **Underlying Assets**: Avoid concentrating your positions in a few individual stocks or ETFs. Spread your exposure across a variety of underlying assets.

3. **Strategies**: Utilize a mix of options strategies with varying risk profiles. For example, combine income-generating strategies like covered calls with directional strategies like long calls or puts.

4. **Time Horizons**: Consider options with different expiration dates to spread your risk over time. This can help manage the impact of short-term volatility.

5. **Correlation**: Be aware of the correlation between your options positions. Diversification is most effective when assets or strategies have low or negative correlations.

6. **Risk Management**: Establish portfolio-level risk management rules. For example, limit the total risk exposure of your options portfolio to a percentage of your overall trading capital.

7. **Regular Review**: Periodically review your options portfolio to ensure that it remains diversified and aligned with your trading objectives. Make adjustments as needed.

8. **Market Conditions**: Adjust your diversification strategy based on current market conditions and your outlook. For example, during uncertain times, you may favor strategies that provide downside protection.

In conclusion, options position sizing and portfolio diversification are essential components of risk management in options trading. Proper position sizing helps limit individual trade risk, while portfolio diversification spreads risk across assets and strategies. Traders should align their risk tolerance, account size, and market outlook with these risk management principles to enhance their chances of long-term success in options trading.

Stop-Loss and Take-Profit Orders

Stop-loss and take-profit orders are vital tools in options trading that help manage risk and lock in profits. These order types provide traders with predetermined exit points for their options positions, ensuring discipline and risk control. In this chapter, we will explore stop-loss and take-profit orders, how they work, and their importance in options trading.

Stop-Loss Orders:

A stop-loss order is an instruction placed with a broker to sell an options position when the price of the underlying asset reaches a specified level, known as the "stop price." Stop-loss orders are primarily used to limit potential losses on options positions. Here's how they work:

1. **Setting a Stop Price**: The trader determines the stop price at which they are willing to exit the trade to limit potential losses.

2. **Activation**: When the market price of the underlying asset reaches or surpasses the stop price, the stop-loss order is triggered.

3. **Market Order**: Once triggered, the stop-loss order becomes a market order, and the broker executes the order at the prevailing market price. It's important to note that the execution price may differ from the stop price, especially in rapidly changing markets.

4. **Risk Control**: Stop-loss orders help traders control risk by ensuring that losses are limited to a predefined amount.

Take-Profit Orders:

A take-profit order is an instruction placed with a broker to sell an options position when the price of the underlying asset reaches a specified level, known as the "take-profit price." Take-profit orders are used to lock in profits at a predetermined level. Here's how they work:

1. **Setting a Take-Profit Price**: The trader determines the take-profit price at which they want to exit the trade to secure profits.

2. **Activation**: When the market price of the underlying asset reaches or surpasses the take-profit price, the take-profit order is triggered.

3. **Market Order**: Once triggered, the take-profit order becomes a market order, and the broker executes the order at the prevailing market price.

4. **Profit Protection**: Take-profit orders help traders protect their gains by ensuring that profits are realized at a predefined level.

Importance of Stop-Loss and Take-Profit Orders in Options Trading:

1. **Risk Management**: Stop-loss orders are essential for managing risk by preventing significant losses on options positions. Traders can set stop-loss levels based on their risk tolerance and trading strategy.

2. **Discipline**: These orders enforce trading discipline by automating the exit process. Emotional decision-making, such as holding onto losing positions or being too greedy with profits, is minimized.

3. **Capital Preservation**: Stop-loss orders help protect trading capital from substantial declines due to adverse market movements.

4. **Profit Lock-In**: Take-profit orders allow traders to secure profits when the market reaches their desired price target, preventing potential reversals from eroding gains.

5. **Flexibility**: Traders can adjust stop-loss and take-profit levels as market conditions change or as the position moves in their favor.

6. **Time Management**: These orders are particularly useful for traders who cannot monitor the markets constantly, as they provide predefined exit points.

7. **Risk-Reward Ratio**: Implementing stop-loss and take-profit orders helps traders maintain a favorable risk-reward ratio in their trading strategies.

Considerations for Stop-Loss and Take-Profit Orders:

1. **Volatility**: Consider the volatility of the underlying asset when setting stop-loss and take-profit levels. Highly volatile assets may require wider price ranges for these orders.

2. **Time Horizon**: Align your stop-loss and take-profit levels with your trading time horizon and objectives.

3. **Market Conditions**: Adjust these orders based on the prevailing market conditions, such as news events or significant price gaps.

4. **Position Sizing**: Ensure that your position size is consistent with your risk tolerance and the stop-loss level you set.

5. **Review and Adjustment**: Regularly review and adjust your stop-loss and take-profit orders as the market evolves and your outlook changes.

In summary, stop-loss and take-profit orders are essential risk management tools in options trading. They help traders limit potential losses and secure profits by automating exit points. Properly setting and adjusting these orders based on risk tolerance, market conditions, and trading objectives is crucial for successful options trading.

Greeks-Based Risk Management

Greeks-based risk management in options trading involves understanding and using the Greeks—parameters derived from an option pricing model—to assess and manage the risks associated with options positions. The Greeks provide insights into how an option's price is likely to change under various market conditions. In this chapter, we will explore how the Greeks—Delta, Gamma, Theta, Vega, and Rho—can be utilized for effective risk management in options trading.

1. Delta: Managing Directional Risk

⟐ **Definition**: Delta measures the rate of change of an option's price in response to a change in the price of the underlying asset.

⟐ **Risk Management Application**:

⟐ **Delta Hedging**: Adjust the position's delta to make it neutral to price movements in the underlying asset, reducing directional risk.

⟐ **Directional Bets**: Manage delta to align with your market outlook, balancing bullish and bearish positions for a desired net delta.

2. Gamma: Managing Delta Sensitivity

⟐ **Definition**: Gamma measures how much an option's delta is likely to change for a one-point move in the price of the underlying asset.

⟐ **Risk Management Application**:

⟐ **Gamma Scalping**: Adjust positions to maintain a desired gamma level, capitalizing on price movements to generate additional profits.

⟐ **Gamma Risk Limitation**: Manage positions to control gamma exposure, preventing excessive sensitivity to delta changes.

3. Theta: Managing Time Decay

⟐ **Definition**: Theta measures the rate at which an option's value declines with the passage of time, also known as time decay.

⟐ **Risk Management Application**:

◈ **Income Generation**: Focus on strategies that benefit from time decay, such as selling options to collect premiums.

◈ **Avoid Excessive Theta**: Be cautious of strategies with high negative theta, as they may incur substantial losses due to time decay.

4. Vega: Managing Volatility Risk

◈ **Definition**: Vega measures the sensitivity of an option's price to changes in implied volatility.

◈ **Risk Management Application**:

◈ **Vega Hedging**: Adjust positions to neutralize vega exposure, particularly when expecting changes in implied volatility.

◈ **Volatility Outlook Alignment**: Tailor positions to benefit from an expected increase or decrease in volatility based on market analysis.

5. Rho: Managing Interest Rate Risk

◈ **Definition**: Rho measures the sensitivity of an option's price to changes in interest rates.

◈ **Risk Management Application**:

◈ **Interest Rate Considerations**: Evaluate rho's impact in relation to prevailing interest rates and adjust positions accordingly.

◈ **Hedging against Rate Changes**: Manage positions to mitigate the risk associated with potential interest rate fluctuations.

Considerations for Greeks-Based Risk Management:

1. **Integrated Approach**: Utilize a holistic approach considering all Greeks and their interactions to comprehensively manage risk.

2. **Portfolio-Level Analysis**: Assess the aggregate Greeks of your entire options portfolio to ensure a balanced risk profile.

3. **Regular Monitoring and Adjustments**: Continuously monitor the Greeks of your options positions and adjust them as needed to align with your risk management goals.

4. **Understand Limitations**: Be aware of the assumptions and limitations of the Greeks in various market conditions.

5. **Educational Resources**: Invest time in learning about the Greeks and how they impact options pricing and risk.

By incorporating the Greeks into your options trading strategy, you can effectively assess and manage risks associated with different options positions, optimizing your risk-return profile. Understanding the interplay of Delta, Gamma, Theta, Vega, and Rho empowers you to make informed decisions, adjust your positions as market conditions evolve, and enhance your overall risk management approach.

Managing Margin and Leverage

Managing margin and leverage is a critical aspect of risk management in options trading. Both margin and leverage play pivotal roles in determining the capital requirements, potential returns, and risks associated with options positions. In this chapter, we will delve into the importance of managing margin and leverage effectively in options trading.

Understanding Margin in Options Trading:

Margin refers to the collateral or funds that traders must deposit with their brokers to cover potential losses on options positions. Options trading involves two types of margin:

1. **Initial Margin**: This is the amount of capital required to open an options position. It ensures that traders have enough funds to meet potential obligations if the options contract is exercised.

2. **Maintenance Margin**: Maintenance margin is the minimum amount of capital that must be maintained in the trading account to keep an options position open. If the account's equity falls below this level, the broker may issue a margin call.

Importance of Managing Margin:

1. **Capital Allocation**: Proper margin management ensures that traders allocate sufficient capital to support their options positions without overcommitting.

2. **Risk Control**: Adequate margin coverage helps control the risk of substantial losses in the event of adverse price movements.

3. **Margin Calls**: By maintaining margin requirements, traders avoid margin calls, which can lead to forced position liquidation and additional costs.

4. **Trading Flexibility**: Effective margin management allows traders to take advantage of trading opportunities with confidence, knowing they have the necessary funds.

Understanding Leverage in Options Trading:

Leverage is a feature of options trading that allows traders to control a larger position with a relatively smaller amount of capital. It amplifies both potential gains and losses. Leverage is achieved through the use of options premiums, which represent the cost of the options position.

Importance of Managing Leverage:

1. **Risk Amplification**: Leverage magnifies both profits and losses, making it crucial to use it judiciously to avoid excessive risk.

2. **Position Sizing**: Proper leverage management helps determine the appropriate position size based on risk tolerance and capital availability.

3. **Risk-Reward Assessment**: By understanding the leverage applied to a position, traders can assess the risk-reward profile more accurately.

Risk Management Strategies for Margin and Leverage:

1. **Position Sizing**: Determine the size of your options positions based on your risk tolerance and the maximum loss you are willing to accept. Avoid overcommitting capital to a single trade.

2. **Stop-Loss Orders**: Implement stop-loss orders to limit potential losses on each trade. Factor in leverage when setting stop-loss levels.

3. **Diversification**: Spread your options positions across different underlying assets or strategies to reduce concentration risk.

4. **Education and Training**: Invest in education to understand the intricacies of margin and leverage in options trading. Familiarize yourself with the rules and regulations set by your brokerage.

5. **Risk Assessment**: Continuously assess the risk associated with your options portfolio, considering the impact of margin and leverage.

6. **Regular Monitoring**: Regularly review your options positions to ensure they remain in compliance with margin requirements and your risk management strategy.

7. **Brokerage Policies**: Understand your brokerage's policies regarding margin and leverage, including margin call procedures.

Effective management of margin and leverage is fundamental to successful risk management in options trading. By understanding these concepts, aligning them with your risk tolerance and trading objectives, and implementing appropriate risk management strategies, you can optimize your options trading performance while safeguarding your capital from undue risk.

Tail Risk Protection with Options

Tail risk refers to the potential for extreme and unexpected events that can result in significant losses in financial markets. Options can be powerful tools for mitigating tail risk, providing insurance-like protection against adverse market moves. In this chapter, we will explore how options can be used to protect against tail risk and safeguard investment portfolios.

Understanding Tail Risk:

Tail risk events are rare but can have a substantial impact on investment portfolios. These events include market crashes, geopolitical crises, economic shocks, and black swan events. Tail risk protection aims to minimize losses during such extreme events.

Using Options for Tail Risk Protection:

Options provide several strategies to protect against tail risk:

1. **Put Options**: Buying put options on individual stocks or equity indices allows investors to profit from a decline in prices. This provides a form of insurance against market downturns.

2. **Long-Term Put Leaps**: Long-term equity anticipation securities (LEAPS) are long-dated put options that offer extended protection against prolonged market declines.

3. **Tail Risk Strategies**: Tail risk strategies involve the purchase of out-of-the-money (OTM) put options to profit from significant market declines. These strategies can be expensive but offer substantial protection.

4. **Collar Strategies**: Collar strategies involve buying protective put options while simultaneously selling covered call options. This provides downside protection at a reduced cost, though it limits upside potential.

5. **Tail Risk Hedging Portfolios**: Investors can construct portfolios with dedicated tail risk hedges, using options to offset potential losses in the event of extreme market moves.

Benefits of Tail Risk Protection with Options:

1. **Capital Preservation**: Options can help protect capital during market crashes or severe downturns, preserving wealth.

2. **Peace of Mind**: Investors gain peace of mind knowing that their portfolios are insulated against tail risk events.

3. **Hedging Flexibility**: Options offer a range of strategies, allowing investors to tailor their protection to their risk tolerance and objectives.

4. **Reduced Portfolio Volatility**: Tail risk protection can reduce the overall volatility of a portfolio, making it more resilient during turbulent times.

Considerations for Tail Risk Protection:

1. **Cost**: Purchasing options, particularly out-of-the-money options, can be costly. Consider the trade-off between cost and protection.

2. **Strategy Selection**: Choose the tail risk strategy that aligns with your portfolio and risk tolerance. Tailor the strategy to your specific objectives.

3. **Portfolio Impact**: Assess how tail risk protection may affect the overall performance and return potential of your portfolio.

4. **Holding Period**: Determine the duration of the tail risk protection. Some strategies may provide short-term protection, while others offer longer-term coverage.

5. **Review and Adjust**: Continuously evaluate and adjust your tail risk protection strategy as market conditions and your investment goals evolve.

In conclusion, options can serve as effective tools for tail risk protection in investment portfolios. Whether through purchasing put options, implementing collar strategies, or constructing tail risk hedging portfolios, investors can enhance their resilience against extreme market events. By carefully selecting the right strategy and balancing cost and protection, investors can safeguard their capital and achieve greater peace of mind in turbulent financial markets.

Chapter 9: Exotic Options and Advanced Strategies

Barrier Options (Knock-In and Knock-Out)

Barrier options, specifically knock-in and knock-out options, belong to the category of exotic options and introduce additional complexity compared to standard options. In this chapter, we will explore barrier options, how they work, and advanced strategies associated with them.

Understanding Barrier Options:

Barrier options derive their name from the presence of a "barrier" price level in relation to the underlying asset's price. These options come in two primary varieties: knock-in and knock-out.

1. **Knock-In Options**:

◈ In a knock-in option, the option only becomes active or "knocks in" when the underlying asset's price reaches a predetermined barrier level.

◈ If the barrier is reached, the option holder gains the right to buy (in the case of a call) or sell (in the case of a put) the underlying asset at the specified strike price.

2. **Knock-Out Options**:

◈ In a knock-out option, the option is "knocked out" or becomes worthless if the underlying asset's price reaches a predetermined barrier level.

◈ If the barrier is touched or crossed, the option ceases to exist, and the holder loses the right to buy (in the case of a call) or sell (in the case of a put) the underlying asset at the strike price.

Advanced Strategies with Barrier Options:

1. **Straddle with Barrier Protection**:

◈ Combining a long straddle with a knock-out barrier option can create a straddle with downside protection.

◈ If the underlying asset's price moves significantly in one direction, the knock-out barrier can limit losses while allowing potential gains from volatility.

2. **Directional Trading with Knock-In Options**:

◈ Traders can use knock-in options to express a directional bias while reducing premium costs compared to traditional options.

◈ For example, a trader expecting a sharp upward movement might use a knock-in call option with a barrier set slightly above the current price.

3. **Hedging with Knock-Out Options**:

◈ Investors holding a portfolio of assets can use knock-out options to hedge against adverse price movements.

◈ By purchasing knock-out put options with a barrier set below the portfolio's value, investors can protect their portfolio while limiting hedging costs.

4. **Volatility Trading with Double Barrier Options**:

◈ Double barrier options have both knock-in and knock-out levels.

◈ Traders can use double barrier options to capitalize on expected volatility within a specified price range.

Considerations for Barrier Options:

1. **Barrier Level Selection**: Choosing the appropriate barrier level is crucial. It should align with your market outlook and risk tolerance.

2. **Premium Costs**: Barrier options often have higher premium costs compared to standard options due to their additional features. Evaluate whether the benefits outweigh the costs.

3. **Market Volatility**: Be aware of market volatility, as it can impact the likelihood of the barrier being touched or crossed.

4. **Monitoring**: Continuous monitoring of the underlying asset's price is essential when trading barrier options, especially knock-ins, to take timely action.

5. **Portfolio Integration**: Consider how barrier options fit within your overall investment portfolio and risk management strategy.

In conclusion, barrier options, including knock-in and knock-out options, are exotic options with unique features that provide advanced strategies for traders and investors. These options can be employed to express specific market views, protect portfolios, and manage risk in a tailored manner. However, due to their complexity and premium costs, it is important to thoroughly understand their mechanics and carefully consider their use within your trading or investment approach.

Binary Options

Binary options are a straightforward yet unique form of exotic option that has gained popularity for its simplicity and potential for quick returns. In this chapter, we will explore binary options, how they work, and considerations for trading them.

Understanding Binary Options:

Binary options are named for their binary, or "yes/no," nature. They offer two possible outcomes:

1. **Call Option**: If you anticipate that the price of the underlying asset will rise above a predetermined strike price by a specified expiration time, you buy a binary call option. If your prediction is correct at expiration, you receive a fixed payout. If it's incorrect, you lose the initial premium.

2. **Put Option**: If you anticipate that the price of the underlying asset will fall below a predetermined strike price by a specified expiration time, you buy a binary put option. If your prediction is correct at expiration, you receive a fixed payout. If it's incorrect, you lose the initial premium.

Key Features of Binary Options:

1. **Fixed Payouts**: Binary options offer fixed payouts, typically expressed as a percentage of the initial premium. These payouts are known before entering the trade.

2. **Expiration Time**: Binary options have a predefined expiration time, ranging from minutes to days or longer.

3. **Predetermined Strike Price**: The strike price is set when you enter the trade and represents the level at which the binary option becomes profitable (in-the-money) or not (out-of-the-money).

4. **Simplicity**: Binary options are easy to understand, making them accessible to traders with varying levels of experience.

Binary Options Trading Considerations:

1. **Market Analysis**: While binary options are simpler than traditional options, they still require market analysis. Conduct thorough research and analysis to inform your binary options trades.

2. **Risk-Reward Ratio**: Assess the risk-reward ratio of each binary options trade. Since the potential loss is fixed, consider whether the potential gain justifies the risk.

3. **Expiration Timing**: Choose an expiration time that aligns with your market outlook. Shorter expiration times may require more active monitoring.

4. **Broker Selection**: Carefully select a reputable binary options broker with transparent terms and fair pricing.

5. **Risk Management**: Implement risk management strategies, such as position sizing and diversification, to protect your capital.

6. **Regulatory Environment**: Be aware of the regulatory environment for binary options trading in your jurisdiction, as regulations can vary.

7. **Scams and Frauds**: Beware of fraudulent schemes and scams in the binary options industry. Exercise caution and conduct due diligence when choosing a broker.

Binary Options as Speculative Tools:

Binary options are often used as speculative tools for short-term trading. Traders and investors should approach them with a clear understanding of the potential risks and rewards. Due to their simplicity and limited duration, binary options can be attractive for those seeking to capitalize on short-term market movements.

In conclusion, binary options are a unique form of exotic option that offers a simplified approach to trading based on binary outcomes. They are accessible to a wide range of traders but require careful analysis, risk management, and awareness of regulatory considerations. Binary options can be used as speculative tools for short-term trading, but it's essential to approach them with a well-informed strategy and understanding of the risks involved.

Asian and Lookback Options

Asian and lookback options are exotic derivatives that differ from standard options in their payout structures and pricing mechanisms. In this chapter, we will delve into the intricacies of Asian and lookback options, how they work, and the strategies associated with them.

Understanding Asian Options:

Asian options, also known as average price options, are derivatives whose payoff depends on the average price of the underlying asset over a specified period rather than the asset's spot price at expiration. There are two primary types of Asian options:

1. **Asian Call Option**: The holder of an Asian call option has the right to buy the underlying asset at the average price over the specified period.

2. **Asian Put Option**: The holder of an Asian put option has the right to sell the underlying asset at the average price over the specified period.

Key Features of Asian Options:

1. **Averaging Period**: Asian options consider the average price of the underlying asset over a defined period, such as days, weeks, or months.

2. **Pricing Averages**: Asian options are priced based on the average of the underlying asset's prices over the averaging period.

3. **Reduced Volatility Impact**: The averaging mechanism in Asian options can reduce the impact of short-term price fluctuations compared to standard options.

Understanding Lookback Options:

Lookback options, also referred to as hindsight options, have payoffs that depend on the extreme price movements of the underlying asset during the option's life. There are two primary types of lookback options:

1. **Lookback Call Option**: The holder of a lookback call option has the right to buy the underlying asset at the lowest price observed during the option's life.

2. **Lookback Put Option**: The holder of a lookback put option has the right to sell the underlying asset at the highest price observed during the option's life.

Key Features of Lookback Options:

1. **Pricing Based on Extremes**: Lookback options are priced based on the lowest (for call options) or highest (for put options) price of the underlying asset over the option's life.

2. **Elimination of Timing Risk**: Lookback options eliminate timing risk, as the holder can exercise at the most advantageous price during the option's life.

Advanced Strategies with Asian and Lookback Options:

1. **Volatility Trading**: Traders can use Asian options to capitalize on anticipated changes in volatility, as these options are less sensitive to short-term price fluctuations.

2. **Portfolio Protection**: Lookback options can be used to protect a portfolio from extreme price movements, providing insurance against unfavorable market conditions.

3. **Tail Risk Management**: Asian and lookback options can be integrated into tail risk management strategies to mitigate the impact of extreme market events.

Considerations for Trading Asian and Lookback Options:

1. **Averaging Period**: Understand the averaging period for Asian options and the impact it has on the option's pricing and sensitivity to underlying asset movements.

2. **Lookback Windows**: Consider the lookback window for lookback options, as it affects the extremes used in the option's pricing.

3. **Cost Analysis**: Assess the premium costs of Asian and lookback options, as they can vary based on the averaging or lookback mechanisms.

4. **Market Conditions**: Consider market conditions and the anticipated behavior of the underlying asset when trading these options.

5. **Risk Management**: Implement risk management strategies to protect capital, as trading exotic options involves unique risks.

In conclusion, Asian and lookback options are exotic derivatives with distinctive payout structures and pricing mechanisms. Traders and investors can use these options for various purposes, including volatility trading, portfolio protection, and tail risk management. It is essential to have a clear understanding of the averaging or lookback mechanisms, premium costs, and market conditions when incorporating these options into trading strategies.

Compound and Chooser Options

Compound and chooser options are sophisticated derivatives that offer unique flexibility and payout structures. In this chapter, we will explore compound and chooser options, how they work, and the strategies associated with them.

Understanding Compound Options:

Compound options, also known as composite or split options, are options on other options. They involve two layers of options: the primary option (known as the "first option") and the secondary option (known as the "second option"). There are two primary types of compound options:

1. **Call on Call (CoC) Option**: This compound option gives the holder the right to buy a call option (the first option) at a predetermined strike price, which in turn provides the right to buy the underlying asset at another strike price (the second option).

2. **Put on Put (PoP) Option**: This compound option gives the holder the right to buy a put option (the first option) at a predetermined strike price, which in turn provides the right to sell the underlying asset at another strike price (the second option).

Key Features of Compound Options:

1. **Two Levels of Strikes**: Compound options involve two strike prices—the strike price of the first option and the strike price of the second option.

2. **Flexibility**: Compound options offer flexibility to the holder to decide whether to exercise the first option (the right to buy or sell another option) and then whether to exercise the second option (the right to buy or sell the underlying asset).

3. **Cost Considerations**: The price of a compound option is influenced by various factors, including the strike prices of both the first and second options and market conditions.

Understanding Chooser Options:

Chooser options, also known as "delayed start" options, provide the holder with the flexibility to choose the type of option (call or put) and the strike price after a predetermined delay or at a specific future date. There are two primary types of chooser options:

1. **Call Chooser Option**: The holder of a call chooser option has the right to choose whether to convert the option into a call option at a predetermined strike price after the delay period.

2. **Put Chooser Option**: The holder of a put chooser option has the right to choose whether to convert the option into a put option at a predetermined strike price after the delay period.

Key Features of Chooser Options:

1. **Delayed Decision**: Chooser options provide the holder with the flexibility to make an informed decision about the type of option (call or put) and the strike price after a specified delay.

2. **Strategic Adaptation**: Chooser options allow investors to adapt their options positions based on changing market conditions or new information.

Advanced Strategies with Compound and Chooser Options:

1. **Risk Management**: Compound options can be used for risk management by providing strategic flexibility in uncertain market conditions.

2. **Earnings Plays**: Chooser options can be used by traders looking to make strategic bets on the outcome of corporate earnings reports, allowing them to adapt their positions based on the report's impact.

3. **Strategic Flexibility**: Both compound and chooser options can be integrated into complex strategies that take advantage of changing market dynamics.

Considerations for Trading Compound and Chooser Options:

1. **Cost Analysis**: Assess the cost of compound options, considering both the first and second option's strike prices and premium costs.

2. **Decision Timing**: Understand the timing of decision-making in chooser options and consider how market conditions may evolve during the delay period.

3. **Market Conditions**: Consider how market conditions and expected events may influence your decision to exercise compound or chooser options.

4. **Risk Management**: Develop strategies for managing risk and adapting your options positions based on your outlook and objectives.

In conclusion, compound and chooser options offer traders and investors unique flexibility in managing risk and adapting to changing market conditions. Compound options involve two layers of options with different strike prices, while chooser options provide the flexibility to make decisions about option type and strike price after a delay. These options can be used strategically in complex trading approaches but require a deep understanding of their mechanics and potential costs.

Exotic Option Trading Strategies

Exotic option trading strategies involve the use of complex and non-standard options to achieve specific trading objectives. These strategies can offer unique opportunities and flexibility but require a deep understanding of the exotic options involved. In this chapter, we will explore various exotic option trading strategies and their applications.

1. **Straddle with Digital Options:

◈ Combine a long straddle (buying a call and a put at the same strike price and expiration) with digital options (binary options).

◈ This strategy benefits from high volatility. If the underlying asset experiences significant price movement, the digital options can provide fixed payouts, while the straddle captures unlimited profits.

2. **Ratchet Options for Upside Leverage:

◈ Use ratchet options, which adjust the strike price upward as the underlying asset's price rises.

◈ This strategy allows you to benefit from strong upward movements in the underlying asset while protecting against potential downside risk.

3. **Rainbow Options for Diversification:

◈ Rainbow options are options linked to multiple underlying assets.

◈ This strategy can be used to create diversified positions that benefit from price movements in various assets within a single option.

4. **Quanto Options for Currency Risk Management:

◈ Quanto options are designed to protect against currency exchange rate fluctuations.

◈ This strategy is useful when trading assets denominated in different currencies, as it allows you to hedge currency risk.

5. **Chooser Options for Adaptive Strategies:

◈ Implement chooser options, which provide the flexibility to choose the type of option (call or put) and the strike price after a delay.

◈ This strategy enables you to adapt your options position based on changing market conditions or new information.

6. **Lookback Options for Extreme Price Movements:

◈ Utilize lookback options, which offer payoffs based on the highest (for put options) or lowest (for call options) price of the underlying asset during the option's life.

◈ This strategy can be employed when anticipating significant price movements and wanting to benefit from extreme prices.

7. **Barrier Options for Volatility Trading:

◈ Incorporate barrier options (knock-in or knock-out) into volatility trading strategies.

◈ These options can be used to profit from expected volatility within specified price ranges.

8. **Compound Options for Strategic Flexibility:

◈ Integrate compound options (call on call or put on put) into complex trading strategies.

◈ This strategy provides strategic flexibility and can be used for risk management in uncertain market conditions.

9. **Asian Options for Averaging Strategies:

◈ Employ Asian options (average price options) when seeking to capitalize on price averages over specific time periods.

◈ This strategy can reduce the impact of short-term price fluctuations.

10. **Binary Options for Short-Term Speculation:

◈ Trade binary options for short-term speculation on the direction of asset prices.

◈ This strategy offers simplicity and rapid outcomes, making it suitable for short-term trading.

Considerations for Exotic Option Trading Strategies:

1. **Advanced Knowledge**: Exotic option trading strategies require advanced knowledge of option mechanics and their pricing.

2. **Risk Management**: Implement robust risk management strategies, including position sizing and stop-loss orders, to protect capital.

3. **Cost Analysis**: Assess the cost of implementing exotic option strategies, including premium costs and potential transaction expenses.

4. **Market Analysis**: Conduct thorough market analysis to inform your strategy and align it with your trading objectives.

5. **Regulatory Considerations**: Be aware of regulatory requirements and considerations related to exotic options trading in your jurisdiction.

In conclusion, exotic option trading strategies offer traders and investors a wide range of tools to achieve specific trading objectives, whether it's profiting from volatility, managing currency risk, or capitalizing on extreme price movements. These strategies provide unique opportunities but require expertise and careful consideration of costs and risks.

Chapter 10: Practical Application and Case Studies

Real-World Option Trading Examples

In the final chapter of this book, we will delve into real-world option trading examples to illustrate the practical application of option strategies. These case studies will provide insights into how options can be used to achieve specific financial goals and navigate various market conditions.

Case Study 1: Hedging with Protective Puts

Scenario: An investor holds a substantial portfolio of tech stocks and is concerned about potential downside risk in the technology sector due to an upcoming earnings season.

Strategy: The investor decides to implement a protective put strategy to hedge against potential losses in their portfolio. They purchase out-of-the-money put options on a technology sector ETF that closely tracks the performance of their portfolio holdings.

Outcome: As the earnings season unfolds, and if the technology sector experiences a downturn, the protective puts provide insurance. The losses in the portfolio are partially offset by gains in the put options, helping to protect the investor's overall wealth.

Case Study 2: Generating Income with Covered Calls

Scenario: A retiree has a portfolio of dividend-paying stocks and is seeking to enhance their income stream.

Strategy: The retiree chooses to implement a covered call writing strategy. They sell call options on their existing stock holdings, effectively granting someone else the right to buy those stocks at a specified strike price.

Outcome: The retiree earns premiums from selling the call options, boosting their income. If the stock prices remain below the strike prices, the calls expire worthless, allowing the retiree to retain both the stocks and the premiums collected.

Case Study 3: Capitalizing on Earnings Volatility with Straddles

Scenario: A trader anticipates significant price movements in a particular stock due to an upcoming earnings announcement but is uncertain about the direction of the move.

Strategy: The trader decides to employ a long straddle strategy by simultaneously buying a call and a put option with the same strike price and expiration date.

Outcome: After the earnings announcement, the stock experiences a sharp price movement. Since the straddle captures gains from both upward and downward price movements, the trader profits from the volatility, regardless of the direction.

Case Study 4: Leveraging Price Trends with Bull Call Spreads

Scenario: A trader identifies a stock with a strong bullish trend and expects further price appreciation.

Strategy: The trader employs a bull call spread strategy by buying a lower strike call option and simultaneously selling a higher strike call option with the same expiration date.

Outcome: If the stock continues to rise, the lower strike call option profits, while the sold higher strike call option limits the overall cost of the trade. The trader benefits from the stock's upward momentum while managing costs.

Case Study 5: Risk Management with Collar Strategies

Scenario: An employee holds a significant amount of company stock options as part of their compensation package and is concerned about potential downside risk.

Strategy: The employee constructs a collar strategy by simultaneously purchasing protective put options and selling covered call options on their company stock.

Outcome: The collar strategy provides downside protection through the purchased put options while generating income through the sale of covered call options. This risk management approach helps the employee safeguard their wealth.

These real-world option trading examples demonstrate the practical application of various option strategies to achieve specific financial objectives, whether it's protecting a portfolio, generating income, capitalizing on volatility, or managing risk. By understanding the mechanics of these strategies and considering their suitability in different scenarios, investors and traders can effectively utilize options as versatile financial instruments.

Case Studies of Successful Option Traders

These traders have demonstrated the power of options in generating profits and managing risk in various market conditions.

Case Study 1: Paul Tudor Jones - The Macro Trader

Background: Paul Tudor Jones is a legendary hedge fund manager known for his macro trading approach. In 1987, he famously predicted the Black Monday stock market crash and profited immensely from it.

Option Strategy: Jones frequently used options to hedge and speculate in the futures and commodities markets. He used put options to protect his portfolio during market downturns while maintaining upside potential.

Outcome: His strategic use of options allowed him to navigate volatile markets successfully. His timely use of puts in 1987 played a pivotal role in protecting his fund from the crash's devastating effects.

Case Study 2: Nassim Nicholas Taleb - The Black Swan Trader

Background: Nassim Nicholas Taleb is a former options trader and author known for his work on risk and uncertainty. He is famous for advocating the use of option strategies to hedge against "black swan" events—unpredictable and extreme market events.

Option Strategy: Taleb employed complex option strategies such as "barbell" and "antifragile" approaches. These strategies involve buying deeply out-of-the-money put options while simultaneously investing in high-risk, high-reward assets.

Outcome: Taleb's strategies allowed him to profit from rare and extreme events, as demonstrated during the 2008 financial crisis. He used his option positions to protect his portfolio against significant losses while benefiting from market turmoil.

Case Study 3: Andrew Hall - The Oil Trader

Background: Andrew Hall is a prominent commodities trader who specializes in oil markets. He is known for his ability to generate substantial profits from oil trading.

Option Strategy: Hall used options to manage risk in the highly volatile oil market. He employed strategies like covered calls and collars to protect his positions while participating in oil price gains.

Outcome: Hall's disciplined use of options helped him navigate the oil market's ups and downs successfully. His ability to protect his profits during oil price declines contributed to his long-term success.

Case Study 4: Karen Bruton - The Options Income Trader

Background: Karen Bruton, also known as the "Options Queen," is a retail trader who gained recognition for her options income trading strategies.

Option Strategy: Bruton specialized in selling options, primarily put and call spreads. She focused on collecting premium income by betting on price stability and used options to generate consistent returns.

Outcome: Bruton's income-oriented options strategies provided her with a steady source of income. Her disciplined approach to risk management and trade selection contributed to her success as a retail options trader.

Case Study 5: Jim Simons - The Quantitative Trader

Background: Jim Simons is a mathematician and founder of Renaissance Technologies, one of the world's most successful quantitative hedge funds.

Option Strategy: Renaissance Technologies employs sophisticated quantitative models that incorporate options trading. They use options to manage risk, generate alpha, and enhance overall portfolio performance.

Outcome: Simons and his team have achieved extraordinary returns over the years, with options playing a role in their quantitative trading strategies.

These case studies highlight the diverse ways successful traders and investors have utilized options to achieve their financial goals. From managing risk to profiting from market anomalies, these traders demonstrate the versatility and effectiveness of options in various trading environments. While their approaches may differ, the common thread among these traders is a deep understanding of options and a strategic use of these instruments to navigate complex markets.

Building and Managing an Options Trading Portfolio

In this chapter, we will explore the process of building and effectively managing an options trading portfolio. Managing an options portfolio involves careful consideration of strategies, risk management, and continuous monitoring. We will outline key steps and considerations for traders and investors looking to create a successful options trading portfolio.

Step 1: Define Your Trading Objectives

◈ *Risk Tolerance*: Determine your risk tolerance, which will influence the types of strategies you employ and the size of your positions.

◈ *Financial Goals*: Clearly define your financial goals, whether they involve income generation, capital preservation, or aggressive growth.

Step 2: Select Appropriate Strategies

◈ *Strategy Selection*: Choose options strategies that align with your objectives. Options strategies can vary from income generation (covered calls) to speculation (long straddles) or risk management (protective puts).

◈ *Diversification*: Consider diversifying your options strategies to reduce risk. Combining strategies can provide a balanced approach to managing an options portfolio.

Step 3: Risk Management

◈ *Position Sizing*: Determine the appropriate position size for each trade. Avoid over-concentrating in a single position, as this can expose you to excessive risk.

◈ *Stop-Loss Orders*: Implement stop-loss orders to limit potential losses on positions. Determine stop-loss levels based on technical analysis, volatility, or other relevant factors.

Step 4: Continuous Monitoring and Adjustment

◈ *Market Analysis*: Continuously monitor the financial markets and the specific assets underlying your options positions. Stay informed about economic news and events that can impact your trades.

◈ *Portfolio Rebalancing*: Regularly review and rebalance your options portfolio to ensure it aligns with your objectives. Adjust positions as market conditions change.

Step 5: Record Keeping and Analysis

◈ *Trade Journal*: Maintain a trade journal to record the details of each options trade, including entry and exit points, rationale, and outcomes.

◈ *Performance Analysis*: Analyze the performance of your options portfolio regularly. Assess which strategies are working well and which may need adjustments.

Step 6: Risk Mitigation

◈ *Diversification*: Diversify your options positions across various assets, sectors, or strategies to reduce single-stock or single-strategy risk.

◈ *Hedging*: Consider using options to hedge existing positions in your portfolio, especially if you have concentrated stock holdings.

Step 7: Adaptation to Market Conditions

◈ *Volatility Awareness*: Be aware of changes in market volatility and adapt your options strategies accordingly. High volatility may favor strategies like straddles, while low volatility may favor income-generating strategies like covered calls.

◈ *Earnings Season Preparations*: Prepare for earnings seasons by assessing the potential impact on your portfolio. Consider implementing strategies that protect against adverse earnings-related moves.

Step 8: Education and Resources

◈ *Continuous Learning*: Stay informed about options trading by continuously educating yourself. Books, courses, and online resources can provide valuable insights.

◈ *Professional Advice*: Consider seeking advice from financial advisors or professionals with expertise in options trading, especially if you are new to options.

Step 9: Emotional Discipline

◈ *Emotion Control*: Keep emotions in check when trading options. Fear and greed can lead to impulsive decisions. Stick to your predetermined strategies and risk management rules.

Step 10: Review and Adapt

◈ *Regular Review*: Periodically review your options trading portfolio and overall financial goals. Adapt your strategies as your objectives or market conditions change.

By following these steps and considerations, you can build and manage an options trading portfolio that aligns with your financial goals and risk tolerance. Options trading offers a wide range of strategies, and successful portfolio management involves a combination of strategy selection, risk management, ongoing analysis, and adaptation to changing market conditions.

Taxation and Reporting for Options Traders

Understanding the taxation and reporting requirements for options traders is crucial to ensure compliance with tax laws and optimize your trading strategy. In this chapter, we will delve into the taxation aspects specific to options trading and outline reporting considerations.

1. Tax Treatment of Options Transactions

◈ **Capital Gains**: Profits from options trading are generally treated as capital gains. These gains can be classified as short-term or long-term, depending on the holding period of the options.

◈ **Short-Term vs. Long-Term**: Short-term capital gains are typically taxed at higher rates than long-term gains. The holding period for long-term status varies by jurisdiction.

◈ **Wash Sale Rule**: Be aware of the wash sale rule, which disallows the immediate repurchase of the same or substantially identical securities within 30 days of realizing a loss. This rule can impact tax deductions.

2. Taxation of Specific Option Strategies

◈ **Covered Calls**: Premiums received from selling covered calls are generally treated as short-term capital gains, regardless of the holding period of the underlying stock.

◈ **Protective Puts**: The cost of purchasing protective puts can be considered a deductible insurance expense for tax purposes.

◈ **Income Strategies**: Strategies focused on generating income, such as writing covered calls or cash-secured puts, may result in short-term or long-term capital gains, depending on the holding period.

3. Tax Reporting Requirements

◈ **Form 1099**: Most brokers provide Form 1099-B, which summarizes your options trading activity, including proceeds and cost basis. Use this form to report your transactions on your tax return.

◈ **Form 8949**: You may need to use Form 8949 to report your capital gains and losses in detail, especially if there are discrepancies or additional information required beyond what is on Form 1099.

◈ **Schedule D**: Include Schedule D with your tax return to report your capital gains and losses. Separate short-term and long-term gains and losses.

4. Tax-Efficient Trading Strategies

◈ **Tax-Loss Harvesting**: Consider tax-loss harvesting by strategically realizing losses to offset gains. This can help reduce your overall tax liability.

◈ **Long-Term Holding**: If possible, aim to hold options and underlying assets for the long term to benefit from lower long-term capital gains tax rates.

◈ **Tax-Efficient Investments**: Explore tax-efficient investment vehicles like exchange-traded funds (ETFs) and tax-managed funds to minimize tax consequences.

5. Tax Professional Assistance

◈ **Consult a Tax Professional**: Due to the complexity of options taxation, consider working with a tax professional or accountant who specializes in securities trading. They can help you navigate tax laws and optimize your tax strategy.

6. Record Keeping

◈ **Maintain Detailed Records**: Keep meticulous records of all your options transactions, including dates, prices, and any related expenses. This documentation is crucial for accurate tax reporting.

7. State Tax Considerations

◈ **State Tax Laws**: Be aware of state-specific tax laws, which can vary widely. Some states may have no income tax, while others may impose additional taxes on capital gains.

8. Estimated Taxes

◈ **Estimated Tax Payments**: If you expect to owe a substantial amount in taxes due to your options trading, consider making estimated tax payments to avoid underpayment penalties.

9. Stay Informed

◈ **Tax Law Changes**: Stay informed about changes in tax laws, as they can impact the taxation of options trading. Tax laws can change from year to year.

It's essential to approach options trading with a clear understanding of the tax implications and reporting requirements specific to your jurisdiction. Staying compliant with tax laws and optimizing your tax strategy can significantly impact your overall returns as an options trader. Consulting with a tax professional or accountant experienced in options trading can be invaluable in this regard.

Current Trends and Future Developments in Options Trading

Options trading is an ever-evolving field, influenced by market dynamics, technological advancements, regulatory changes, and investor preferences. Staying informed about current trends and anticipating future developments is crucial for options traders and investors. In this chapter, we will explore the latest trends and potential future developments in options trading.

Current Trends in Options Trading:

1. Increased Retail Participation:

◈ The rise of commission-free trading platforms and easy access to options has led to a surge in retail options trading. Retail traders now play a more significant role in options markets.

2. Growth in Complex Strategies:

◈ Options traders are increasingly employing complex strategies involving multiple legs, such as iron condors, calendar spreads, and ratio spreads, to capitalize on market volatility and generate income.

3. Algorithmic and High-Frequency Trading:

◈ Algorithmic trading and high-frequency trading (HFT) have gained prominence in options markets, enabling rapid execution and liquidity provision.

4. Options on Cryptocurrencies:

◈ The introduction of options contracts on cryptocurrencies like Bitcoin and Ethereum has opened new opportunities for traders looking to hedge or speculate on digital assets.

5. ESG (Environmental, Social, and Governance) Options:

◈ Growing interest in ESG investing has led to the development of options contracts tied to ESG-focused indices and assets, catering to socially responsible investors.

6. Expanded Exchange-Traded Products (ETPs):

◈ The creation of new exchange-traded products, including options on ETFs and ETNs, provides traders with diverse exposure to various asset classes and strategies.

7. Volatility Trading:

◈ Volatility trading strategies, including those using VIX options and other volatility-related instruments, have gained popularity, particularly during market uncertainty.

8. Options Education:

◈ Options exchanges and brokerage firms have invested in educational resources to help traders understand options, offering webinars, tutorials, and options trading platforms with educational tools.

9. Regulatory Changes:

◈ Regulatory bodies continue to review and update options trading rules and regulations to enhance market integrity and investor protection.

Future Developments in Options Trading:

1. Cryptocurrency Options: Continued growth in the cryptocurrency space may lead to the introduction of options contracts on a broader range of digital assets, further integrating cryptocurrencies into traditional financial markets.

2. **Environmental Options**: The focus on environmental issues may lead to the development of options contracts tied to carbon credits and other environmental assets.

3. **Artificial Intelligence (AI) and Machine Learning**: Advanced AI and machine learning algorithms may play a more prominent role in options trading, assisting traders in strategy optimization and risk management.

4. **Enhanced Risk Analytics**: Options trading platforms are likely to offer more sophisticated risk analytics tools to help traders assess and manage their risk exposure effectively.

5. **Regulatory Changes**: Continued regulatory updates may include measures to address market manipulation concerns related to high-frequency trading and ensure transparency in complex options products.

6. **International Expansion**: Options markets may expand globally, with exchanges introducing options on new international indices and assets, increasing cross-border trading opportunities.

7. **Environmental and Social Responsibility**: Options traders may increasingly consider ESG factors when evaluating investments and strategies, leading to the development of ESG-focused options products.

8. **Customization and Structured Products**: Investors and institutions may seek more customized options contracts and structured products to meet specific risk management and investment needs.

9. **Decentralized Finance (DeFi) Options**: The growth of decentralized finance may lead to the development of DeFi options markets, providing alternatives to traditional options trading.

10. Increased Automation: Automation may become more prevalent in options trading, with algorithmic strategies becoming more accessible to retail traders.

Staying informed about these current trends and potential future developments in options trading can help traders and investors adapt to changing market dynamics and seize new opportunities. As the options landscape evolves, flexibility and the ability to integrate these trends into your trading strategy will be key to success in options markets. Additionally, it is essential to stay updated on regulatory changes that may impact options trading practices.

Don't miss out!

Visit the website below and you can sign up to receive emails whenever Alex Thompson publishes a new book. There's no charge and no obligation.

https://books2read.com/r/B-A-FEPY-ERSOC

BOOKS 2 READ

Connecting independent readers to independent writers.

Also by Alex Thompson

Alex on Finance

Financial Freedom Roadmap - Achieving Early Retirement through the FIRE Movement
The Art of Strategic Innovation
Beyond Cash - The Evolution of Digital Payment Systems and the Future of Money
Preserving Wealth in Inflationary Times - Strategies for Protecting Your Financial Future

Standalone

Side Hustle Success: Unlocking Your Entrepreneurial Potential
Side Hustle Success: The Ultimate Guide to Passive and Financial Freedom
Mastering the Markets: Advanced Trading Strategies for Success and Ethical Trading Practices
Financial Fortitude
Mastering the Art of Upselling
The Financial Bullet Blueprint
Investing Demystified: A Beginner's Guide to Building Wealth in the Stock Market
Real Estate Riches: Building Wealth through Property Investment
How To Succeed as a Freelancer

Navigating Complex Waters: Advanced Strategies in Portfolio Management
Behavioral Finance and Investor Psychology
Leading with Empathy: Harnessing Emotional Intelligence for Effective Leadership
Financial Independence
Thriving Within Your Means: A Guide to Affordable Living
Algorithmic Trading: Navigating the Digital Frontier
Navigating Alternative Investments
Navigating the Behavioral Finance Landscape
Unlocking the Power of Derivatives
Mastering International Finance
Quantitative Finance and Risk Modeling
Sustainable and ESG Investing
Options Mastery: Navigating the Financial Frontier
Portfolio Mastery: Navigating the Financial Art and Science

www.ingramcontent.com/pod-product-compliance
Lightning Source LLC
LaVergne TN
LVHW022052200926
848481LV00003B/883
* 9 7 9 8 2 2 3 6 6 1 9 9 3 *